Working with Others

Aspects of Helping & Counselling

(4th Edition)

Bryce Taylor

Oasis Publications
Beechwood Conference Centre, Elmete Lane, Leeds. LS8 2LQ

First edition published   1986
Second edition published   1989
Third edition published   1992
Fourth edition published   1995

TAYLOR, BRYCE 1946
Working with Others
Aspects of Helping and Counselling
1. Counselling
2. Training

ISBN 187199 2 060

Designed and Printed by Maxiprint Colour Printers, York.

DEDICATION

This book is dedicated to the many
hundreds of participants who have
taught me what I have come to know
about training others in counselling
skills in the introductory workshops
I have led over the last ten years.
To them all thanks.

I hope this goes some way to clarifying
the many dilemmas they have raised
in that time.

Bryce Taylor

CONTENTS

Preface

There is considerable and increasing interest on the part of many people involved in the helping or 'caring' professions in the role that counselling and counselling skills can play in promoting the interpersonal effectiveness of helpers. **Counselling, however, is only one particular form of helping relationship** that can be distinguished from a range of others. The value of counselling as the **appropriate** strategy to employ with any individual or group will depend upon the purpose of the help being offered, the problem under review, and the preferred method and skills of the helper. Most people attending counselling courses are not necessarily looking to become psychological counsellors, working with individuals on a long-term basis to produce therapeutic change. Rather, they are aiming to increase the range of their understanding of counselling approaches and the skills employed in counselling and its application to other helping activities in what may be termed their 'guidance role'.

Section I

Helpers & Helping

Chapter One

Helping as an Activity

Many factors influence what goes on when one person helps another or when a group meet and overcome some difficulty. Whatever we would like to believe about our own motives as helpers, the first issue for any helper to acknowledge is **'What's in it for me?'** Helping others serves the helper's needs, whether it be the need to feel satisfied at a job well done, or appreciated by an individual who has succeeded in some task they have previously failed. Helping is not an exclusively altruistic activity and helpers have needs of their own. Unless helpers are clear about their needs, they can suffer from over-work, exhaustion and the phenomenon of 'burn-out' which is indicated by a loss of commitment. Because helping is a very demanding activity, helpers stand in danger of being open to exploitation and manipulation either by clients or by the organisations which employ them. This may not be out of any deliberate or conscious intent but more likely out of the expectation that the helper must respond to anyone at any time. Perhaps the most important skill for helpers is to establish satisfactory personal boundaries to ensure they have time for themselves, time to recuperate and time to take stock.

What Helpers Need

The desire to help another is no guarantee of success.

All forms of helping, including counselling, are essentially applied activities; mere **knowledge alone is not sufficient to make an effective helper**. The key is the ability to apply knowledge sensitively and appropriately to facilitate an individual or group toward the resolution of some dilemma. Consequently, a helper's main resource for their work is themselves. The more they understand about themselves, and the greater self-awareness they possess, the less likely it is that they will become subject to any of the many pitfalls there are to effective helping. **Self-awareness** is an all embracing term to describe a group of inter-related aspects of self-other understanding. There appears from research (Avila, Combs and Purkey, 1977) to be six major elements of self-awareness that contribute towards making an effective helper and in developing one's own resource strength. These are set out below. The term used to describe helping activities which rely upon the use of self as the major resource is the **self-as-instrument.**

Knowledge

Helpers need to have a sound understanding of the underpinning rationale for whatever kind of help they are offering. Intuition and playing hunches can sometimes be a potent source of assistance, but are not a sufficient basis for offering systematic, purposeful and aware help to others. For individuals coming into a helping role without prior training, acquiring a sound understanding of the effective limits to their helping role can take a considerable time and cause much uncertainty and anxiety. It is important for helpers to take time to discuss their views and increase their understanding of how they can help, what help they can legitimately provide, and perhaps most importantly, why they are being seen as a helper in the first place. Experience in such matters is no alternative to training. Opportunities to share issues and concerns with others in a similar role is an essential need for developing a sound understanding of what they are there to do.

Frame of Reference

All people in a helping role act upon some basic assumptions they have acquired, often unconsciously, about the nature of the world in which they live, the rights and responsibilities of people, and how they regard helping as an activity. If these assumptions are based upon a need for control and direction for their own good, and a need for assistance in making the right choices, then these assumptions will find their way into the helper's way of responding. If, however, the frame of reference of the helper is one that generally regards human beings as essentially trustworthy, able to achieve growth and change and overcome difficulties, they will operate from a different value position. An individual's 'frame of reference' is often not easy to identify, least of all for the person themselves, yet it influences all that they think and do. It provides people with their ready-made view of the world which they bring to any situation they find themselves in.

How people behave at any particular moment is a result of how things seem to them. Helping people achieve more satisfying ways of living and being is therefore a matter of **facilitating change in what people think and believe about themselves and their world.** To do this well, effective helpers need to understand the nature of personal meaning and how the individual's view of the world can be widened and enriched.

Views of What People Are Like

Helpers are influenced by their views about what people are really like. An attitude toward others in difficulty that respects the dilemmas they face, and offers support without taking over the problem, will communicate itself to the individuals seeking help. Some assumptions that suggest such an attitude are:

* People are essentially worthy of dignity and respect.
* People can resolve their own predicaments if given support of the right kind, and will do it better than others, since they got themselves into the predicament to start with.
* People can work together positively.
* People have an inherent capacity to work, learn, grow and mature.

Helper's Self-concept

An individual's self-concept is not a 'thing', but an original set of ideas, perceptions and values that attach to an individual's sense of self. It extends to cover one's loved ones and possessions, such as when my friend becomes upset when I thoughtlessly put aside a piece of 'junk' which he later tells me is his latest product at his art class. Our sense of self becomes invested in our relationships with others, so that we come to feel keenly the distresses they experience and the satisfactions that accompany their achievement.

Self-concept represents what people perceive themselves to be and what they believe themselves to be. For helpers it is especially important to investigate and understand their own self-concept in order to increase their awareness of the motivations and beliefs influencing them in offering help to others. If helpers have a self-concept which is categorised by low self-esteem, for example, if they believe themselves to have little to offer, then they may be in the helping business to earn the gratitude of those they help.

People who are seeking help are often at their most vulnerable and have to overcome the embarrassment and insecurity of admitting they need outside assistance. This may make them easily dependent on the helper and may lead them to see the helper as some kind of wise and all-powerful mother or father-figure able to make things right. A helper who is looking to earn gratitude from their clients may easily succumb to such appeals, and run round doing things and putting the client's world right in order to secure the praise clients can readily give, never realising, until too late, that such activity only fosters the dependency of the client upon the helper.

A helper's self-concept will influence very considerably how far they set out to encourage a client to move toward a genuine **independence, autonomy and freedom of choice,** and so will affect how successful they are as a helper. Individuals who have examined themselves, who have seen something of the discrepancies **between how they would like to think they are and how they really are,** and **who can accept themselves** with all their imperfections, are likely to be more effective in encouraging others who are struggling with the same process. The more helpers learn to accept themselves, the more, it seems, they are able to accept others, and the more able those people are to accept themselves. Self-acceptance, however, is not to be mistaken for complacency or making a virtue out of any shortcomings.

Purpose

Helpers must take account of their activity in relation to the purpose they set for themselves, in relation to the purpose of the setting in which they find themselves, in relation to the time available and the wider purpose of the society in which they exist, as well as in relation to the purposes the client may have. These can be difficult issues to integrate together harmoniously, and many helpers have to learn to live with **high levels of ambiguity** about what they do and how far the limits of their involvement should extend. Since most people involved in helping do so only as part of some wider role, this issue can be particularly acute. A willingness to do one's best to help another may well begin to reveal dimensions of difficulty that the helper is under-equipped to deal with, and that the organisation is unprepared to accept, with too little time to handle any of it constructively. The results can be distressing, or worse, for all concerned. Training courses where such issues can be explored in the company of others facing similar issues can help inexperienced helpers begin to understand the complexities of their dilemmas and to learn that there are no simple answers.

In acute cases where the ambiguity between the purpose of the organisation and the purpose of the helper is too wide, helpers may well leave to seek a setting within which to operate that is more in keeping with their own values and beliefs.

Helping Methods and Techniques

Gerard Egan (1975) says that ineffective help is not something neutral: it can have positively damaging effects. It may reinforce the individual's belief that no-one really will listen, and therefore lead them to avoid looking for help elsewhere, or it may help precipitate an avoidable crisis. Helpers, therefore, need to have a repertoire of methods, techniques and skills at their command, and be able to use them with **deliberate and aware choice.** It is not possible to know the effects of interventions before they are made, but it is important to recognise the likely areas of enquiry which certain skills will open for examination. Skills to help others can be acquired with training and practice.

Chapter Two

A Helping Framework

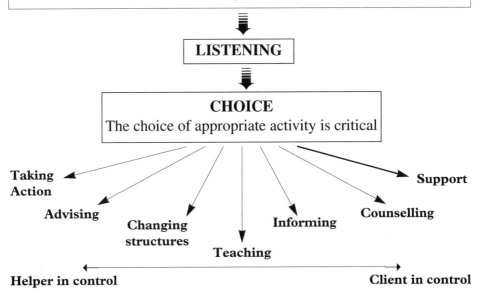

AIM OF HELPING
To promote increasing self reliance, choice and personal responsibility

**The helping process is
mediated through a relationship based on:**
Openness
Equality of worth
Trust
indicated by RAPPORT

LISTENING

CHOICE
The choice of appropriate activity is critical

Taking
Action

Advising

Changing
structures

Teaching

Informing

Counselling

Support

Helper in control

Client in control

Helping and Control

If you look at the framework reproduced above it becomes apparent that the further to the left hand side of the spectrum a helper operates from the more they retain the initiative and the power. As you move towards the right, control gradually pushes towards the client until with **Support** control is unilaterally with the client. Helpers would therefore be wise to ask themselves if they can really deliver the goods if they offer to support someone because the implication is that it is "OK to be where you are for as long as you want to be there". You, as a helper may feel that way towards the client, but your agency may well have expectations that they will see results. The resulting **role conflict** can put great strain on the helper and the helper-client relationship. Qualified support however, is in almost every case worse since you never know how far it extends or for how long it will last. Better to work out a realistic arrangement of what you can offer one another than pretend time is limitless if it is not.

Strategies

Helpers need a range of strategies upon which to draw. Some are easier to implement than others and some take more time than others, all helpers have preferences for some strategies over others. The setting, too, influences the options available and may pressurise the helper into relying upon speed of response at the expense of accuracy of understanding.
The differing strategies can be thought of in the following ways:

* **Taking Action**
  The helper decides on the course of action to be followed and executes it on behalf of the client.

* **Advising**
  The helper gives an explicit recommendation to the client of a course of action the client should follow.

* **Changing Structures**
  The helper shifts the focus away from the client and attempts to improve the structure within the helping system itself to enable the client to be better served in the future.

* **Teaching**
  The helper takes the time to provide a joint problem-solving approach that enables the client to take increasing responsibility for themselves in the future.

* **Informing**
  The helper offers up-to-date information relevant to the client's present need.

* **Counselling**
  The helper offers a relationship to the client for the purpose of enabling the client to change.

* **Support**
  The helper is available to the client on an unconditional basis for the client to seek refuge. This is rarely a feasible strategy for a professional helper since they are paid to make a difference and bring about change. Support is valued precisely because there are no expectations to live up to.

The choice of strategy is crucial. The helper must find the best 'fit' or 'blend' of helping approaches to meet the client's needs and the situation in which they meet.

The more the client is in control, the more the helper works with the client – **teaching, informing or counselling** – the more the solutions are likely to be developmental. The less the client is in control the more likely it is that the solutions will be remedial. All these strategies are explored more fully in the next chapter.

Helping Styles, Strategies and Problems

With the exception of counselling, the remaining strategies assume that the individual's needs are clearly known and have advanced to a stage where a specific activity is both necessary and appropriate. In practice this may not always prove to be the case: a fact which underlines the importance of taking time to review the situation in order to accurately understand the nature of the real problem before any of the above activities may be undertaken. This is an important and over-riding helping skill. A particular problem may well require elements drawn from a number of activities in order for it to be resolved. For example, in order to leave college, a student may require **counselling** to discover if such is the decision. They may also need **information** about alternative options, jobs, voluntary work, and so on, and may feel the need to be **taught** new skills to enable them to cope with new situations.

Helping and Counselling

One reason why **counselling skills** as opposed to **counselling training** is widely used in the preparation of a very wide variety of helping professions is because at the heart of counselling is two essential ingredients. Firstly the importance of **effective listening skills**, and secondly the communicating of the core conditions of **respect, empathy, and genuineness**.

All helpers need to learn to listen or they will end up solving the wrong problem! So practice in counselling skills can be a beneficial development in the training of a **first-in-line helper**.

In considering any strategy, as we have already indicated, the nearer the left-hand side of the fan on page 14, the more the helper is in control and directing the way help is provided. The more a helper moves to the right, the more the client is in control of the helping process.

Thus in a counselling relationship the balance is very clearly in favour of the client, who decides: the **level of disclosure**, the **extent of willingness to explore an issue**, and **whether or not to attend future sessions**. Helpers should be very clear in their own mind when they move into such a relationship that they have genuinely accepted the amount of direction offered to the client in counselling.

A further factor influences the helper's choice of approach when dealing with problems and that is their own preferred style. There are, for example, helpers who have little interest in exploring the nuances and ambiguities of any issue but who are highly effective in mobilising resources and getting things done. Helpers need to recognise their preferred style and to understand something of its strengths and limitations before they find themselves repeatedly and unthinkingly applying a single strategy which may be inappropriate to some situations.

Referral

Referral is not separately distinguished within the range of helping strategies illustrated in the fan on page 14. Rather than being seen as one particular skill, referral is better regarded as an underlying resource which needs to be available irrespective of any particular strategy. For **first-in-line** helpers (as in the following chapter) knowing the extent of their involvement with those in difficulty is only part of the information required to work within their boundaries effectively.

They also need to learn the appropriate referral agencies and the contact persons within these agencies who they are most likely to rely upon. Identifying local agencies alone is rarely enough to make referral an effective step in helping someone. Referral takes place when a client is presenting difficulties or experiencing dilemmas that are **beyond the ability of the agency or its helpers to cope**. There are therefore high levels of insecurity around for everyone. Clients are likely to experience further insecurity at the thought of having to retell their story all over again to someone else. And the thought of being so 'odd' that they need yet another type of help than the one already offered may discourage them from going to someone else.

Such circumstances are not the best for the staff of one agency to attempt to make contact with those of another for the first time. This is a separate task which requires to be undertaken in preparation for such a crisis and not at the same time. It is very often the informal, personal links between staff from different agencies that make all the difference in effecting the smooth transition of the client from one agency to another.

Opportunities for individuals from different agencies to meet their respective contacts generally receive too little encouragement by the host agencies, and yet the pay-offs can be immense in the improved effectiveness of the help offered and in efficient use of the time and status of the people involved.

Chapter Three

Types of Help

Offering help to another may take a number of forms. In practice a particular problem may require elements of several of these forms, but they are distinguishable and each have certain costs and benefits worth noting. Seven main types of helping are distinguished here:-

(i) *Taking Action*

The helper initiates a piece of action intended to alleviate the person's predicament - for example, undertakes to represent him or her at a hearing, write a letter on his or her behalf, make a telephone call, etc.

Costs

* The individual may not learn how and why the helper chooses to act in a particular way.

* If the problem recurs, the client may have few extra skills or resources to bring, and may revert automatically to seeking the 'expert' again.

Benefits

* Action is prompt, and the problem is usually dealt with swiftly.

* If the 'expert' is well-chosen and can be relied upon to know the 'best' course of action, the problem is solved.

* The 'helper' recognises the limits of the time, skills, etc. it would require to solve the problem for themselves.

(ii) *Advice Giving*

The helper makes a suggestion based on knowledge and understanding of the person and problems, and allows the individual to decide on its appropriateness.

Costs

* If it is considered and rejected, the adviser can come to feel rejected and refuse further help.

* It is difficult to estimate the full consequences to someone else of any course of action recommended.

* The adviser does not have to live with the consequences of any suggestion.

* There is a danger of advice being given prematurely - it may only serve to solve the wrong problem.

* Giving advice is very easy to do badly and very difficult to do well

Benefits

* It can cut through a lot of confusion.

* It can help the individual to see a way forward without forcing them to take the preferred suggestion.

* It can be particularly useful when there is professional expertise involved: for example, over specific issues such as legal and financial matters, housing etc.

(iii) *Changing Systems*

The helper alerts the system, whether it be a group, an office, a factory, school, hospital or other organisation of issues that individuals are repeatedly encountering. This implies that the predicaments of some individuals are best resolved through changes to the system, or to its procedures, rather than through changing the individual. If 24 students leave a course in two years, this suggests there is something wrong with the course or its selection procedures, and that it is these that should be altered rather than the students.

Costs

* Systems are not easy to confront: who does the helper negotiate with?

* Negative information is often not heard constructively by organisations.

* The role of change agent requires considerable skills and access to sources of influence and ultimately of power.

* Individuals who seek to change systems can sometimes risk having their career in the organisation blocked.

* Change agents are often regarded as disrupters and a nuisance to stability.

Benefits

* Improved organisational effectiveness is likely to improve morale.

* Responsiveness by the organisation to the people it serves increases their commitment.

* Change has positive outcomes for all if handled constructively.

(iv) *Teaching*

The helper manages a learning experience or structures a situation in order that the individual might improve his or her knowledge, acquire new skills, or develop insights further.

Costs

* It takes time to establish 'real' learning needs.

* It can be experienced as oppressive to the learner.

* Experts can seem to wish to retain their own sense of separateness and to keep knowledge to themselves.

* Learning skills and transferring them to a new situation is not easy, and teaching often makes it look easier than the individual discovers it is in practice.

Benefits

* It recognises the need to plan for a solution and does not expect it to appear by chance.

* Once a skill has been acquired or information gained, it can be used repeatedly.

* Individuals can be helped to plan their own learning programmes.

* It takes a developmental view of difficulties rather than a crisis approach.

(v) *Information Giving*

The helper provides a piece or pieces of data based on evidence, gives accurate accounts of facts and figures, and generally offers reliable sources of information, without recommending any as having more or less value than another.

Costs

* Not much information can be presented without suggestions being made as to how it should be used, in which case it becomes advice.

* It requires good inter-agency contacts to make the most of information services.

* The relationship with clients is usually of a short span - it is not always possible to diagnose 'real' needs, as opposed to those the client admits to having, in such a short time.

* It can mean the individual has to seek help at another agency and tell their story all over again.

Benefits

* It leaves the client to decide; it is relatively value free.

* Information services can be relatively cheap to run and can cope with large numbers of enquiries.

* It can make the most of helpers who have no great amount of training.

(vi) *Counselling*

One way of defining counselling is that it consists of **'offering a relationship to another for the purpose of change'**.

The helper works with the individual's 'internal dissension' through the relationship offered. Where other types of help rest on making an effective enough relationship with the client to move to the task in hand and solve the problem, counselling is both the means and the method. It is, then, through the relationship itself that the problem becomes identified, acknowledged, worked with and, hopefully, resolved. Counselling is therefore a task which requires high levels of commitment to provide appropriate support to those in difficulty, a consistent way of relating, and some measure of internal self-discipline and supervision. Since no-one knows all that goes on between two people, opportunities to review a session are an integral part of monitoring performance and deepening both the skills and the insights of the counsellor. Counselling implies a process of encouraging individuals to confront their dilemmas and difficulties in a supportive framework of trust, safety and acceptance.

Costs

* It is often a lengthy process.
* It is very easy to do badly.
* The predicament has to be one appropriate for counselling.
* Counsellors can be asked to 'save' others from themselves and they can also be asked to 'save' colleagues (or 'difficult' students, customers, staff).

Benefits

* It enables people to 'own' their inner difficulties and overcome them.
* Growth and change are inherently challenging - counselling can provide support to assist such growth and change.

* Some experienced difficulties require a strong, stable and supportive relationship if they are to be resolved.

* It encourages accurate communication at both a content and feelings level.

(vii) *Support*

Support is the least directive form of help offered by one person to another. It is more often associated with the informal interest of friends and neighbours than viewed as a deliberate strategy of a helper. However, non-judgemental support, or the knowledge that there is someone there who will first listen and only listen, can be a vital resource for someone moving towards accepting the reality of a difficult situation.

Costs

* Support can be very demanding if limits and boundaries are not discussed.

* Support can amount to little more than 'collusion', helping the client stay where they are.

* Support can generate a mutual dependency between helper and client.

Benefits

* Support leaves the client in control.

* Support enables a client to have a haven of security where they are not being asked to answer for themselves.

* Support can be a very powerful form of reassurance.

Chapter Four

Who Are The Helpers

There are many people who offer help as an incidental part of their work. There are others for whom it is an essential part, nursing, for example. But for a great many people helping is a part of what they do and has to be accommodated into a wider set of constraints and responsibilities.

First-in-line Providers

Helping is an important part of the role of certain specialists - social workers, nurses, teachers, etc., but it is not the exclusive preserve of any. It is open to all of us to offer our help in whatever way we feel right for us throughout our daily lives. Frequently it is the case that the individual with **first-in-line** responsibility for staff in an organisation - the supervisor, the foreman, the teacher, the ward sister or charge nurse - will be the first-in-line point of contact for a member of staff meeting difficulties. This raises immediate problems.

Most such staff with first-in-line responsibilities have a contrasting role to that of helper to their staff. They are also **boundary managers.** They have a function in setting and maintaining clear boundaries of action and conduct. It is often felt that these two aspects of the role are in conflict - as indeed they are - and therefore incompatible, which need not be the case.

Such **role-conflict** is not unique to helpers, but it can be an acute problem for them. It will often be the case that an individual who needs help will be performing below their usual level of competence and may well be presenting problems of attendance or discipline as a symptom of their current difficulties. This places both the client and the first-in-line helper in something of a dilemma unless they are careful. Whenever a person is invited to explore an issue where such role relationships exist, the first-in-line helper should set out from the beginning the nature of the meeting they are to have and leave the client with no room for uncertainty about the purpose they have come together to fulfil. If the meeting is a fact-finding exploratory discussion, this should be made clear and it should stay in that territory. If it is really a means to challenge an individual to improve their performance, it should equally be made clear, and if it is to offer a person a genuine opportunity to begin to unburden themselves of the concerns that are influencing their performance, this again should be made clear.

Specialists

Some organisations have already convinced themselves of the need to have specialist helpers on hand, and view them not as a non-productive use of resources, but as valuable contributors to maintaining the overall effectiveness and morale of the staff.

Clearly, if the tasks of the first-in-line provider are to be performed skilfully, then there will be a need for some form of support. This is an important role for specialists, who may themselves not have direct contact with clients throughout their working time, but who may act in a consultancy, advisory and support role to first-in-line providers and undertake a proportion of internal referrals. Such specialists are also in key positions to negotiate not only across the internal boundaries of the organisation in which they work, but also across external boundaries with other agencies. This makes them well placed for coordinating helping activities within their organisation and between their organisation and relevant referral agencies.

Confidentiality

Clarity of purpose must be accompanied by the discipline of maintaining confidentiality of information given. Information gained in a counselling session should not be made available to other staff without a clear and aware decision and a willingness to give an account of oneself to the client **first** as to why the information should be shared. Nor should such information be used by the same individual in other aspects of their role. If you invite people to confide in you, you need to be able to respect that it may bring you problems but should not add to theirs. Confidentiality is a complex question and is returned to later in this book.

Chapter Five

Helpers and Their Settings

In addition to the personal limitations of helpers themselves and the limitations that arise from lack of experience, training and skills, there is a further set of constraints which can have great influence upon the effectiveness and involvement of potential helpers. These are the constraints imposed by the organisation, the setting and the role within which the helper has to practise.

Organisations and Boundaries

The relationship takes place in some context, a setting which usually make clear the nature of the help that is offered, the purpose the agency serves and what kinds of difficulties are legitimate for its staff to respond to. All helpers operate within a given set of conditions about the time they have available, the style of the meeting they use and what can be offered.

All organisations operate within some set of boundaries or limits which determines the extent of their willingness and ability to respond. Many helpers operate from within organisations whose primary purpose is not the giving of help itself or the solving of individual problems. For example, most industries are established to satisfy needs via products or services. This may mean that the helper is regarded as an essentially non-contributing member of the organisation, and individuals with problems as potential labour operating at less than optimum efficiency. Such a view 'marginalises' the importance of the helper's activities. On the other hand, an organisation that recognises a willingness to respond to the wider needs of its members, as a way of improving the overall working climate, is likely to respect its helpers and offer them access to those who formulate policy. Most organisations come between these two positions and may constantly re-examine how far they are willing to respond to individuals in difficulty according to a variety of internal pressures. Helpers who ignore the purposes of the organisation and who operate in an unsupportive climate may experience loss of interest, commitment and motivation. Trying to help in ways not acceptable to the organisation is a recipe for conflict.

The Setting

Where the helper is located in the organisational environment - whether they are in suitable premises, whether they are a visible member of the organisation - will influence how accessible others find them. The time available and the place in which helper and 'client' meet will have great influence upon what can be accomplished. Many helpers operate in settings that are not conducive to full-scale counselling, and therefore need to 'manage' their contacts with people in difficulties so that they can arrange to make themselves available for the time required. Over-hasty counselling can be worse than no counselling. If it can't be done, do not attempt it. The important thing is to offer real help, not to demonstrate how compassionate you are if it does nothing to help the client.

The Role

How far the setting influences the development of the counselling relationship is an important consideration. The midwife in a home, a manager in the office, a housing benefits worker in an interview rooom all have very different contexts in which their skills, often the same skills, are being used. Similarly, the role relationship between those involved will have a considerable impact.

It is not that the effect of these factors needs to be neutralised so much as to be recognised and acknowledged. If they are not, the individuals involved might well blame themselves in not succeeding at something that is a great deal more to do with the **roles** they play or the context in which they meet rather than **who** they are.

Therefore, the role an individual plays within an organisation will have a great impact upon the helping activities he or she undertakes. Some people occupy roles of considerable ambiguity: on the one hand, they are in a managerial role with all that implies; on the other, they are somehow supposed to act as a supporter to their staff. Sometimes this role conflict is 'resolved' by the individual emphasising one part of the role at the expense of the other, but this is rarely satisfactory. An important helping skill is making clear to those who need to know what boundaries and limits are in operation and what the consequences are of ignoring or disregarding them. Such limit-setting need not be punitive, but helps to create the structure clearly in the minds of those involved.

There are other **role influences** which affect the way in which helpers can operate. **Status and rank** will make the work of some helpers seem more 'un-sympathetic' and so on by others. Helpers can become **'role-stereotyped'** just as other groups can.

Chapter Six

Problems in Helping

Problems for the Helper

The wish to help is not sufficient to ensure success. There are a number of 'blocks' to effective helping and some of them are related to lack of skill, confidence or awareness on the part of helpers themselves. There are three important ways in which help can become degenerate rather than productive as a result of the helper's behaviour. They are: **unsolicited** interventions, **manipulative** help, and **compulsive** efforts on the part of the helper.

Unsolicited Help

Here the helper begins to intervene without first clarifying whether help is being sought and whether they can supply it adequately. This can be a subtle form of interference and can remove from the client important areas of personal decision-making. It is often very difficult to challenge such help out of fear of appearing ungrateful or being accused of being arrogant. Fear of rejection can also play its part in someone going along with this process. Unsolicited help can encourage passivity and dependence and leave the problem little improved.

Manipulative Help

Help that is motivated primarily out of the self-interest of the helper is manipulative. In its extreme, it is the clear, conscious and deliberate making use of others to fulfil our own needs or personal ends.

Compulsive Help

Help that is narrowly restricted to the same set of suggestions or formulae that have been well tried already would suggest compulsive help. Similarly, repeatedly 'fishing' over areas of the client's life that may have abiding interest to the helper but no crucial relevance to the problem is another example of the same process.

Problems for Those Being Helped

It can be a very difficult and painful admission to recognise you can no longer manage your difficulties and need the assistance of someone else. It can be made worse if you feel you really ought to "pull yourself together and get on with it". Other difficulties that many of us experience include being told that we somehow ought not to have the problems we have now admitted to having.

Help v 'Rescuing'

We have so far seen that there are three major influences acting upon helpers. Rarely do these three influences act harmoniously together. Most of the time we are 'helping', there is at least some degree of 'dissonance' or tension between the conflicting demands placed upon the person in the helper role. These three sources of pressure are: **the setting**; **the role**; and **the level of skill** a helper possesses.

Frequently helpers confront dilemmas about the legitimacy of their involvement. How far should they get involved? Have they the skills required? How far do you go in offering support? How do you challenge clients to take some measure of responsibility for what is happening to them? How do you offer support in such a way that it can be rejected if it is not the right time for them and without appearing casual in your concern? How do you approach issues when there might well be a catalogue of painful experiences behind them? And not least; how do you cope with the fact that some clients are dealing with lives that are far more emotionally distressing than anything you have ever experienced yourself?

There are no easy answers to such questions. Establishing appropriate limits which will lead to a satisfactory involvement for all concerned - client, helper and setting - is not easy. In part, the answer lies in the level of skill possessed by the helper. But skills are only the starting-point.

Assuming the role of helper immediately places an individual in a position in which difficult choices still remain to be made about the role appropriate to those skills and to the setting. Designated helpers often feel a tremendous obligation to be doing something because they believe it is expected of them. Equally, the feeling that it is their task to 'solve' all problems places an unrealistic burden of responsibility and later of guilt when problems do not get solved as neatly or as easily as the helper would like. Burn-out amongst helpers is high for these reasons.

It is useful for helpers, therefore, to distinguish between **'Rescuing' or inappropriate attempts to help**, and 'helping' which is a legitimate response to assist another person in difficulty. For those employed in a caring or helping role, the 'Rescuer' position comes all too easily available as a response to the feeling of pressure to be seen to be doing something at the first sign of someone in difficulty. Over time, it can become a patterned response that may well not meet the needs of the situation. 'Rescuing' of this kind has a compulsive quality about it. The client comes to be seen as a 'Victim' and is inadvertently encouraged to become dependent on their 'Rescuer', who gets the things done for them that they cannot do themselves. Far from encouraging self-reliance, such **'Rescuing' perpetuates dependence and exploits the difficulties of the client in order to enable the helper to meet their own needs** - perhaps the need to be seen as a dedicated concerned helper or as skilful problem-solver.

The important question to get straight is to find out if your help is appropriate in the first place. Four questions can help to clarify a decision:

* Is this person able to do without my help?

* Will what I am doing contribute towards their independence?

* Did this person ask for help or accept my offer of help?

* Is there a clear understanding between us about the nature of my help?

Just as **help offered too soon is as ineffective as help offered too late**, so too 'Rescuing' for the helpers' own need to feel they are doing their job has the consequence of removing choice from the client being helped, when increasing choices is the purpose behind offering help in the first place.

Once a client senses that they are being 'Rescued' the way lies open for deception, manipulation and exploitation of the helper. Deception can take the form of pretending the problem is solved to get out of the stifling clutches of someone who may take over your life; manipulation can take the form of praising the helper for being so wonderful so far that "Here's an even bigger problem for you now"; and exploitation can take the form of generating new crises to maintain the helper's involvement in the life of the client whenever the helper suggests it is time to consider terminating the relationship.

Chapter Seven

Stages of Helping

All the forms of help that have been examined so far have a place to play in the overall aim of helping another to achieve constructive change. **Helping is a person-centred activity**. The first priority is to establish accurately the type of help that will most appropriately aid the client: that is, to accurately understand the nature of the predicament. Any type of help is likely to pass through a number of steps in moving toward the solution of the dilemma.

The Essential Steps

Initiating contact: establishing a good working rapport.

Exploration of themes/issues.

Identifying options.

Assisting towards choice and decision.

Such a simple four-stage model of the helping process identifies the importance of **establishing an effective working relationship**, something which takes precedence over everything else. Once it has been established, then an elaboration of the **themes and issues** can begin. This in turn leads toward the **identification of options:** a consideration, say, of the types of help available and the cost and benefits of each. Finally, the stage of **choice** and **decision-making** brings the process towards some closure: a decision to meet to review progress might form part of such a phase.

A Model of Helping

Brammer's model of the helping process breaks down the four stages above into greater detail to give a more precise formulation to the sequence effective help takes. The model is reproduced below, in relation to the four stages discussed here.

A FOUR STAGE HELPING MODEL

The Meeting Phase

* Initiating satisfactory contact.

* Clarifying   : exploring the apparent cause of coming together.

* Constructing   : devising a suitable structure to work in.

* Contracting   : agreeing the boundaries of working together.

* Relating   : developing the helping relationship.

Exploring of Themes and Issues

* Exploring   : outlining the range of the problems.
                       : identifying related issues.
                       : clarifying implications.

* Consolidating   : focusing on areas to work on together.
                       : developing a theme.

* Challenging   : confronting the incongruities.
                       : challenging restrictions and self-imposed limitations.

Identifying Options

* Reviewing   : understanding the ground covered.
                       : reviewing progress.
                       : identifying learning and implication for change.

Assisting Towards Choice and Decision

* Decision-making : outlining options, considering alternatives, devising strategies.

* Implementing   : agreeing action plans.
* Concluding   : closure - drawing the session and ultimately the relationship to an appropriate close.

Section II

Listening and the
Core Conditions of Helping

Chapter Eight

Listening

"A good listening is soothing to the heart". The experience of being really and fully listened to is not as common as most people believe. Most conversations, even with those we know well, do not take place with the full attention of those taking part, and are always open to one or other of the parties changing the subject at any time. Listening is an essential precondition for any type of effective help, and follows quite different ground-rules from normal conversation.

Aspects of Listening

First of all, there is an expectation that the listener will not change the subject, but instead will assist the client to focus more closely on the issues that concern them. There is also an expectation that the helper will give more than superficial attention to what is being said and will not be subject to internal personal distractions of their own. In a very real sense such listening is a self-denying activity and one which requires full attention and concentration.

A critical part of the role of listening in a helping relationship is to create a climate of freedom and openness in which the other person can feel able to disclose to the fullest extent the problems which they are confronting. **Self-disclosure** - the giving away of personally important information - **is a risky activity**, and can touch off concerns about an individual's self-image and worries that they may be being judged for admitting to inadequacies or defects.

Listening in a helping relationship is very closely linked with the ability to establish the core conditions for effective help that have already been identified: genuineness, empathy and warmth. These conditions will be re-examined in some detail later.

Elements of Listening

"If I do not listen well, then I do none of the rest that I am supposed to be doing", said one college counsellor. Accurately hearing what is being described, hearing 'the music behind the words', is an active process which involves overcoming many of our habitual ways of responding when others are talking.

The major barrier to better mutual inter-personal communication is the natural tendency to judge or criticise, to approve or disapprove, what the other person is saying. A good deal of communication resembles a game between those involved. The speaker assumes they are being listened to, and the listener conveys the impression that they are listening and reacting even though, for the most part, they may have 'tuned out'. Such listening has no place in a helping relationship.

The most complete form of listening is not listening to, but listening with another person in an **active and involved way**. This means that we are no longer observers but become active experiencers of what we are being told. Research in communication reveals that listening is a complex form of behaviour involving many skills - skills which can be identified and improved. How well a person **can** listen and how well they do listen are not the same thing. There are numerous factors which influence the quality of the communication between individuals or groups. **The situation itself**, how it was organised, **who organised it**, the **intended purpose of the occasion** and the **eventual outcome** of the meeting, will all influence the involvement of those taking part.

The relationship between a talker and listener is open to mismanagement and manipulation. Information gained in a helping session can be inappropriately used outside such a meeting, with loss of confidence on the part of the client, who may decide never to trust the helper again. The limits of information-sharing should be decided with the client, so that if information is to be taken elsewhere, then they know clearly who it will be shared with and for what purpose.

Messages can be broken up in several ways: in particular, they have a **content** - a meaning - and they also have an **emotional component** - which tells us something of how the speaker feels about what they are saying. This second part, the **affective component**, is conveyed through the non-verbal signals accompanying the message: through the use of such things as tone of voice, facial expression, gestures and so on. Recognising and using such non-verbal cues in order to help the client express fully their concerns is an important part of effective counselling.

Difficulties in Listening

How an individual feels about what they are saying is often more important in establishing what they really mean than what they actually say (content). People who do not know each other well, or who have some reason to be wary or apprehensive of one another, may find it difficult to 'hear' clearly what is being said to them. Anxiety in a listener increases defensiveness and the propensity to misinterpret statements and the tendency to find unintended threats and challenges increases. Supportive encouragement from the listener, with the use of gestures and expressions of encouragement, can help to reduce anxiety and to lead the way to a more open form of communication. Such encouragement indicates to the speaker that they are being listened to and that what they say is being valued. The more space to talk that they are given, in an encouraging way, the more they will be able to explore what they think and feel.

Listening is an active skill which can be learned, changed and developed like any other behaviour.

We all experience the world differently, and our concepts of things rarely match exactly those of anyone else. This may lead to difficulties when listening because we assume that the speaker's meaning matches the one we have. Often this will not be so: their own personal experience of events may have given them a different shade of meaning from that which we possess.

Internal States and Attitudes

How we feel and look upon what we are being told affects profoundly how we respond to it. **What we decide to select out as important** and what we choose to screen out and overlook, influence the way we feel about what happens to us. Being aware of our own prejudices and biases can help us to listen better, but strongly-held attitudes have a pervasive effect upon how we respond. All of us tend to evaluate what we hear far too soon, and once we have made our evaluation, it takes us a long time to give it up. **We become attached to our ideas as much as to anything else, even when they are inaccurate**. There is some evidence to suggest that there are differences in the listening skills of men and women, differences which are in line with our role-stereotypes for each of the sexes. How far this is innately true and how far a matter of cultural conditioning is not clear. Women are regarded as having a more finely developed intuitive grasp of things, whilst men are said to be more rational, logical and so on. Perhaps the most important thing to be gained from such studies is a reminder that we are all inadequate as listeners and all have skills which are in need of development.

The capacity to listen varies from one person to another, and from one day to another, but listening concerns the individual's ability to select and structure what is being presented and to remember it. This will be influenced by such things as intelligence, motivation, familiarity with the subject, and so on.

The willingness to listen is probably as important as the capacity to listen. Some people seem never to listen; others seem to distort whatever they hear. An ability to listen that is never put to use is no good to anyone. Poor listening habits cause many of us to listen much less well than we could. Listening well is an essential skill in any helping relationship.

Most communication is used to influence an individual or an outcome. Therefore defensiveness is always possible on behalf of those involved, and this may make it difficult for them to 'hear' accurately what is being said. Deliberate attempts to coerce, exploit or manipulate the listener will be counter-productive in the long run and will lead to a deterioration in the quality of the relationship. Even with good will assured on both sides, successful communication cannot be guaranteed.

Modes of Listening

Most people use the time during which others are talking to prepare what they are going to say. Although we like to believe that talking and listening goes something like:

YOU SPEAK	I LISTEN
YOU LISTEN	I SPEAK

In truth it is much more like:

YOU SPEAK   I LISTEN
I LISTEN - EVALUATE - LISTEN - PLAN - LISTEN - REHEARSE
- SPEAK
(at the first opportunity I find to stop you)

Even 'good' listeners are often guilty of evaluating critically what is being said before attempting to understand what the speaker is trying to convey. The result is that they often jump to premature conclusions about what the speaker is driving at. This, rather than assisting the flow of communication, only disturbs it. The speaker has to try to explain what he means a second time.

Problems of Listening

We tend to listen least well to the middle of a statement.

Our previous knowledge and expectations may lead to our hearing only what we expect to hear.

Similarly, because of previous knowledge and existing attitudes, we frequently reduce a message by eliminating detail - **in other words, we listen selectively**.

Before the speaker has finished delivering their message, we are already formulating an answer. This means we do not listen to the end of the message, and may even finish off the sentence for them.

Problems for Listeners

There are a number of interventions which do not encourage the talker, but which many listeners find themselves using. Among the most frequent are:-

Inappropriate probing	-'Why exactly do you feel this way?'
Excessive reassurance	-'Everything is going to be O.K.'
Evasion	-'Please don't be upset.'
Evaluation/Judgement	-'You feel upset, but just think how your wife feels.'
Hostility/Judgement	-'Your behaviour is stupid and foolish.'

The aim of effective listening, then, is to allow the client to explore their own feelings in more depth. Only by coming to terms with their own emotions will they be able to cope with and understand new information, or to formulate a policy of action.

Blocks to Listening

There are a number of commonly experienced blocks to effective listening. We have difficulty in hearing the words of another when any of these factors are present:-

* When different value systems exist between helper and client, or when differences in education, experience and class background are present.

* When the vocabulary used by the two parties is very different.

* When either of the parties has an accent or appearance that is extreme in some way.

* When the content is shocking.

* When the helper gets out of their depth.

* When the information offered is not what the helper wants to hear.

* When the helper is distracted by their own internal pre-occupations.

* When judgements of liking or approval are not forthcoming but are being sought or expected.

* When the environment is unsuitable.

Chapter Nine

Core Conditions

Respect or acceptance, **genuineness** or authenticity, **empathy** or appreciation are regarded as the core conditions necessary for effective counselling to be possible.

All person-centred approaches are most effective when the individual offering help is able to establish a sound relationship based on **trust** with the person they are helping. Evidence from research points to there being three core conditions for the establishment of such a relationship.

Truax and Carkhuff (1967) describe these conditions as:

Genuineness: Genuineness represents the helper's successful avoidance of posturing with the client, playing a role or erecting a facade or barrier between themselves and their client.

Empathy: Empathy represents the helper's successful attempt to comprehend their client's thoughts and feelings in the way in which they are comprehended by the client – and to communicate that comprehension.

Warmth: Warmth represents the helper's communication of their willingness to accept and respect the client.

It is essential, therefore to encourage an environment where **RESPECT** or acceptance, **GENUINENESS** or authenticity and **EMPATHY** or appreciation are present in order for effective counselling to be possible.

Respect

In order for someone to enter fully into their dilemma, they have to come to feel that they themselves are not going to be judged as failures. To admit failings is one thing, but many people when they seek help do not believe that they are going to be accepted by the person in whom they are about to confide. 'Respect' is the term used to convey the quality of non-judgemental acceptance offered by a helper to the other person. It is the quality of expressing a genuine regard for the other and a warm dispassionate interest in what the client is attempting to disclose and understand. It is a non-threatening, non-evaluating acknowledgement of the reality and integrity of the client as a person. It needs to be carefully distinguished from a dependent wish to be 'nice' to people or to make excuses for people. It is a realistic, not a sentimental, posture. Rogers (1961) uses the term 'unconditional positive regard' to convey his understanding of this essential component of the helping relationship. It means holding to the belief that the client has the potential to move beyond their current difficulties in a positive and life enhancing way. Rogers explains "It means there are no **conditions** of acceptance, no feelings of 'I like you only if you are thus and so'." Egan (1975) also stresses the importance of regarding the client as unique - another element in the quality of respect - and says that "although they are committed to helping the client change, this does not mean that the helper is determined to make the client over in his own image and likeness". This may mean that ultimately the client will choose a course other than that the counsellor would choose or one which the counsellor thinks is below the most effective available to the client. But the helper will unequivocally respect such choices.

Respect for others forms part of the underlying core of beliefs that effective counsellors and helpers hold. In this sense it is not something simply acquired once and for all, but something to be striven for and developed **both as a belief and as a communicated act** toward those the helper works with.

Genuineness

Genuineness is about risking being real. "It indicates an openness in dealing with others and behaviour that is truly reflective of the core of the being." (Pietrofesa *et al*; 1978). Genuineness is therefore about being at one with oneself, not employing facades. Another term often used in this respect, is 'congruence', and refers to 'transparency' or internal consistency.

The congruence is between what the helper is in reality and what they appear to be to the client: they allow themselves to be known as a real and authentic person. This calls upon resources of honesty and courage on the part of the helper.

These elements are linked to the capacity for **appropriate self-disclosure**: the willingness of the counsellor to display and take responsibility for personal values, ideals, feelings and experiences. Spontaneity also seems linked to this same area of activity, i.e. behaving freely and without constraint.

Such behaviour has the effect of offering a model to the client that such openness to self can be risked without loss of self-acceptance or risking the necessary condemnation of others. But these qualities require a certain level of mature and genuine non-defensiveness in their expression; otherwise they might become little more than the outpourings of the counsellor's own unresolved difficulties. Such 'genuineness' would be likely to offer little therapeutic benefit to the client.

"If the 'counsellor' spontaneously and honestly conveys his thoughts and reactions, I believe they are not only communicating his concern but they are in effect both eliciting and reinforcing kindred uncontrived behaviour." (Jourard, 1964).

When counsellors withhold their 'real selves' some measure of energy is required in order to maintain the deception which this takes away from the therapeutic task. 'Certainly the aim is not for the therapist to express or talk about his own feelings, but primarily that he should not be deceiving the client as to himself. At times he may need to talk about some of his own feelings (either to the client, or to a colleague or superior) if they are standing in the way' (Rogers, 1961).

Avila *et al* writes (1977) "We suggest a major problem of poor helpers is the fact that their methods are inauthentic, that is, they tend to be put on, contrived. As such they can only be utilised so long as the helper keeps their mind on them. That, of course, is likely to be disastrous on two counts. In the first place it separates them from their client or student, and the message conveyed is likely to be that they are not 'with it', are not really interested, or are a phoney. Second, it is almost never possible to maintain attention to the 'right' method for very long. As a consequence, the poor helper relapses frequently into what they believe his previous experience has taught them. So the method they are trying to use fails because of the tenuous, interrupted character of their use of it."

Authentic and Inauthentic Behaviour

Inauthenticity is unhealthy and removes people from experiencing themselves truly.

Inauthentic behaviour makes it very difficult to know 'what's going on' in situations for two reasons. First, it is likely to be assumed that everyone else is as inauthentic as you are, therefore making any accurate interpretation impossible. And second, it is difficult to make even tentative assessments of atmosphere and dynamics if you are out of touch with the instrument you rely upon, i.e. yourself.

Authentic behaviour encourages others to take risks and offers a model of how it might be done.

Spontaneity and self-disclosure are indicators of genuineness.

Genuineness indicates a 'being at home with oneself': an important quality for anyone helping others to experience the same unity.

Self-concealing takes time and energy away from the opportunity of fully developing relationships with others.

Techniques are much less important than the ability to experience and convey genuineness to the client.

Genuineness of itself is not necessarily therapeutic, but without it the therapeutic process is not likely to succeed.

Empathy

In helping others it is not only important to understand what it is the client is saying; it is just as important to communicate such understanding effectively. This is the area of counselling and helping covered by the word 'empathy'. Empathy is not only the ability to listen to and understand the experiences, feelings and beliefs of others: it is also the ability to communicate the understanding and appreciation of these experiences, feelings and beliefs accurately back to the client. Communication at this level helps the client feel understood and therefore freer to express more of their own inner life.

Everyone experiences the world differently and builds up an individual frame of reference. Empathy in counselling is indicated by the counsellor suspending their own frame of reference in order to enter that of the client, attempting to make sense of what the client discusses in the same way that the client does, and making the client aware that this is what the counsellor is doing.

It does seem from studies (Carkhuff, 1971) that people from similar backgrounds are more likely to be empathic to one another than people from widely different backgrounds: blacks, for example, will have more empathy with other blacks, and so on. This might be especially the case on occasions when the counsellor is using their own experience of what a situation is like to guide them toward understanding the effect it has upon a client. The danger of such use of self is that it can be wide of the mark.

Another basis for an empathic response is to offer a 'normative response': to offer a reaction that would be 'typical' of 'most' people in that situation. Here again the danger lies in generalising that what most people might feel, this person actually **does** feel.

To build an empathic relationship, counsellors need to attend very carefully to the variety of clues from the client, both verbal and non-verbal. To make such detailed attention available, the counsellor must be **free from internal preoccupations, external distractions, or defensiveness toward the client**.

The Importance of Empathy

Fielder's work (1950), supported by other research since, indicated that it was the quality of empathy and acceptance communicated to and experienced by the client which had most influence in promoting positive change for the clients, irrespective of the particular theoretical orientation offered. It was not what they knew that made the helpers effective, but how fully they could indicate real understanding for their clients and their difficulties.

The work of Bandler and Grinder (1978) has explored these issues in more detail, and has helped to devise strategies to enable therapists and counsellors greatly to increase their effectiveness through

Neuro-Linguistic Programming (NLP). NLP encourages helpers to establish much more effective levels of contact by alerting helpers to the way in which people make sense of the world through different channels of communication, i.e. visual, auditory, or kinaesthetic (feeling). The ability to recognise which channel a client uses and to respond back in that same channel is a highly effective way of indicating empathy.

Empathy in Practice

An empathic relationship is one in which a counsellor is attempting to explore the client's understanding, rather than the client trying to explore the counsellor's suggestions or advice. The counsellor is not 'taking over' the problem or solving it on their own behalf, but is offering a mutuality of understanding. **The counsellor thus remains outside the dilemma but inside the understandings**, and 'stays with' the pace and tone of the client. The counsellor helps things to emerge - they do not drag them forth or discourage them from appearing. Following on from this, it is clear than an evaluative or judgemental attitude to a client will undermine any empathic building which has taken place.

Empathic responses place a value on the person and give recognition that the individual in difficulty is worthy of care and attention. They help individuals to experience themselves more deeply and therefore more completely. To give this kind of **permission** can have swift and liberating effect. To encourage, for example, a bereaved relative to find, experience and express the accompanying anger at the loss of a loved one, as well as the sadness and longing, can provide an important realisation that such feelings are part of the total process of grieving, though a part that is often overlooked.

Levels of Empathy

There are different degrees of empathy, from simply understanding the content of what someone says, to entering into the complexities of the emotional tone of an experience. The ability to respond accurately to the emotional component of a response requires considerable skills and attentiveness. Depending on the relationship, empathy may be conceived as having four different levels, each one more difficult to model successfully.

Can you tell the client what they just told you?
Can you repeat what is said?

Can you tell the client what they are trying to tell you?
Can you infer what is meant?

Can you tell the client what they would really like to tell you.
Can you infer what the client wants to approach?

Can you tell the client what they are scared to tell you?
Can you pick up the clues and identify the area of experience the client wishes to talk through but feels too scared to begin, and encourage them sensitively to talk?

Suggestions for Indicating Empathy

Be attentive, physically and mentally, to what is happening.
Listen carefully and note the key words.
Respond encouragingly to these core messages - but be willing to move in new ways if indicated.
Be flexible. If what you are doing is not working, try something else.
Give permission for the emotional tone to find expression as well as the content.
Look carefully for cues that you are on target.
Be aware of signs that you are not together and be prepared to change.
It is not clients that are resistant, but counsellors who are not effective in finding the right strategy.

Section III

Aspects of Counselling

Chapter Ten

Counselling as a Helping Relationship

What is Counselling?

Counselling is a word with different meanings for different groups of people who are engaged in a helping or supervisory role with others. Some of the different definitions offered seem to bear little relation to one another. For example, it is not uncommon in the Health Service to find the term 'counselling' associated in many people's minds with part of a disciplinary process as well as with the supportive relationship that a nurse offers a patient! Such incompatible definitions exemplify the very real difficulty in striving to find a satisfactory definition of the extremely complex activity which occurs when two or more people enter a counselling relationship. This is not surprising when you consider that the term can be used to describe a range of activities from giving informal advice to professional consultations. The dictionary is little help either, since the word is linked there with activities including advising and recommending which have more of a prescriptive flavour to them than counselling itself usually implies.

Another factor complicating matters even further arises out of the different backgrounds and training of the various professional groups who employ counselling skills as a part of their working role and who therefore come to associate the core skills and approach of counselling with their own particular style. When professionals from different groups come together to discuss 'What is counselling?' it is not unusual to find competing definitions and claims from each group that their particular approach or their particular method is **the** one which is most representative.

Youth workers, for example, operate in an informal and semi-structured way which allows counselling skills to arise from the activities they stimulate. Not unnaturally they prize the equality of the relationship they offer to young people and the way in which counselling forms part of that relationship. By contrast, probation officers, social workers, and others often have highly structured guidelines in which to operate. This in turn restricts how counselling skills can be employed. Such workers will often emphasise the value of the formal element of counselling for this reason.

Perhaps the most important point to be learned by all concerned is that the setting bears a great influence upon the way that counselling skills are employed and that the structuring of the relationship in which counselling is established is a topic of particular importance (see below).

Defining Counselling

There are two definitions of counselling offered here. The first and simplest reflects the central importance of the **relationship** that makes counselling possible at all. The second is taken from the British Association for Counselling and is used because it attempts to include a range of underlying features held in common by a variety of professional helpers.

Sometimes 'counselling' is used almost synonymously with 'psychotherapy'. The boundary where one ends and the other begins is ultimately almost a matter of nicety of distinction. Long-term counselling might well be indistinguishable from some types of psychotherapy, but for most people using this manual this issue is not likely to arise. If it does, then they would need to consult and read other more advanced texts than the present one.

Definitions

"Counselling is offering a relationship to another for the purposes of change."

"People are engaged in counselling when a person occupying regularly or temporarily the role of counsellor offers or agrees explicitly to offer time, attention and respect to another person or persons temporarily in the role of client." (BAC)

Within this definition counsellors are seen as undertaking to meet a number of professional responsibilities.

Chapter Eleven

Helping The Client: An Overview

Counselling as a Helping Process

Carl Rogers (1961) defines a helping relationship as one in which "one of the participants intends there should come about in one or both parties more appreciation of, more expression of, more functional use of the latent, inner resources of the individual". Such a definition can therefore extend beyond the counsellor-client relationship to include the relationship of parent to child, of doctor to patient, of teacher to student, in fact any relationship which promotes human flourishing.

If counselling works through the medium of the relationship established between those involved, certain implications follow.

A Positive Relationship

Effective help depends upon the ability of the counsellor to establish a positive relationship with the client. (Research indicates that warm egalitarian attitudes by parents towards their children have positive influences in promoting such things as emotional stability and feelings of security, and that therapists achieve better results when viewed as being 'caring' by their clients.)

Responsiveness

In order to facilitate the client through their difficulties, the counsellor must be responsive to the client in difficulties. Dittes, quoted by Carl Rogers (1961), found that any sign of a reduction in acceptance by therapists towards their client was sufficient to lead to an immediate increase in anxiety symptoms, increased heart rate, etc., and to the display of stress signals. One study found a strong relationship between success in therapy and the degree of liking and respect felt between client and their therapist, rather than the particular school of therapy the therapist had been trained to use.

Responsibility

The counsellor accepts responsibility for providing focus, direction and structure to the sessions. The counsellor offers the client certain skills to help bring meaning out of the apparent chaos of their feelings and to assist them towards a clearer understanding of their own world. Fielder (1950), quoted by Rogers (1961), found that what appeared to be most important to successful therapy was the therapist's ability to demonstrate a genuine desire to understand the client's feelings and meanings.

The Client

The client is someone whose world is in turbulence or whose emotions are in conflict. The client experiences the world in which they live as 'Not being as I would like it to be'. They come to the counsellor in the hope or belief that the situation can be changed towards becoming 'More like I want it to be'.

It is not often possible (or desirable) to change the world in which the client lives, but it may well be possible to help the client change the way they experience the world and how they feel about it, not by providing solutions to the client's difficulties but by helping them find their own.

Counselling Groundrules

Counselling works through the medium of the relationship that develops between the client and the counsellor. The fewer obstacles the counsellor puts in the way, the fewer personal concerns they have and the more open and free the attention they offer, the more the client is able to make a real opportunity of the situation in order to explore their fears, concerns or dilemma.

A number of ground rules and suggestions follow from these assumptions:

*The counsellor needs to establish rapport easily and swiftly.

*The counsellor needs to know which behaviours help deepen and extend rapport and **to be willing to use them.**

*The counsellor's task is to enable the client to feel safe enough to talk about those things they wish at a level that is productive.

The qualities that best describe these abilities are:

Acceptance, or Respect: for the client in difficulty.

Appreciation, or Empathy: a willingness to attempt to understand the client from the client's own point of view.

Authenticity, or Genuineness: for the counsellor not to adopt a distancing pose, but to allow for there to be genuine meeting.

Having such qualities is not in itself sufficient to establish the counselling relationship. **It is important to communicate these qualities by behaving in ways that illustrate to the client that you have them.**

Acceptance is indicated by such things as:

*basic courtesy.

*attending and listening carefully.

*creating time and space free from distraction.

*not supplying ready made solutions.

Appreciation is indicated by such things as:

*sharing your understanding of the client's story as it unfolds.

*not jumping to conclusions.

*allowing the client to clarify their understanding through asking questions, seeking information and feelings.

Authenticity is indicated by such things as:

*a readiness to share such aspects of your own life and experiences as are appropriate and relevant to the client's needs.

*withholding from seeking to make use of the relationship for your own needs, but recognising that they exist.

*a willingness to be sensitive to the full that some things people tell you will disturb and upset you and there is no reason to let such reactions get in the way of you being there for the client.

Counselling is a learning process and the client will learn a number of things from the time they spend with you that may seem incidental but will have an impact upon their life. For example:

*the way you help someone solve 'this' problem will help them learn a process they will probably go on to apply to every other problem that has the same structure. **Make sure you teach them well.**

A Model of Counselling

An individual enters the counselling relationship to make sense of some dilemma or to move towards the resolution of some problem, and look to the counsellor to bring their experience and expertise to bear to facilitate that process in a way which combines specific skills and strategies.

Skills

Problems ————> <———— Outcome

Strategies

Contact and Relationship Building

Rapport is about developing a satisfactory relationship in order for change or development to take place. Behaviour which promotes effective rapport includes:

Matching: using language similar to that of the client in non-patronising ways.

Mirroring: offering similar body movements and allying one's body posture towards that of the client.

Pacing: working at the client's speed and being willing to suspend one's own belief system for long enough to help the client identify their own.

A further element in **Rapport** which begins to move the client forward is **leading.**
The counsellor helps the client move from a position where the world "is not as I would like" toward a place where the world is "more like I would like". It is essentially a problem-solving process. It has a pattern and a sequence which can be broadly identified.

Frame of Reference

The problem exists for the client within themselves and their own world. This makes it unique. However much it sounds like another example of something commonplace, to the client it makes sense only in relation to their own internal frame of reference, the values they hold and the difficulties they have already worked with. It takes a long time (rather than a short one) to establish enough of a sense of the client's **frame of reference** to make confident guesses as to what they feel or think. Time spent unravelling and exploring is well spent because you too will be aware of the implications of the options the client is considering.

Clarifying and Listening

The skills the counsellor relies on most frequently are various forms of questioning to fulfil a number of purposes to:

* **gather information.**
* **test understanding.**
* **seek feelings.**
* **summarise.**
* **challenge implications.**
* **encourage action.**

Many of these skills are designed to help the client **clarify** their understanding and to provide a richly detailed description of the internal experiences that are limiting their choices.

Problem Solving and Questioning

The counsellor needs to help the client define the situation and circumstances, to work through the implications and dilemmas and to define the options clearly as well as to act responsibly.

Challenge and Change

Counselling is not always a linear process that follows a simple beginning, middle and end to a session. There are important periods of apparent diversion, moments of insight, times of rambling and scouting around the issue. However there needs to be a **sense of some progression** in any session and a development for both counsellor and client, if they are to feel they have achieved something worthwhile.

Progress and Change

Progress can be defined as change or movement in one of the four following areas:

(i)   *An Increase in Understanding of the Situation*

As a result of counselling, the client may feel little different. The situation may still be as intractable as ever, but the process of speaking out loud has enabled them to discern a thread of meaning which make the circumstances more tolerable. Such growth in **insight** does not necessarily lead to change, but is almost always a precursor to any successful change.

Counselling may help the client come to a greater understanding or appreciation of the complexity of an issue which appeared to be relatively insignificant but incapacitating. Difficulties in relationships with close colleagues, friends or partners are often triggered by what appear to be almost trivial differences. Through counselling, a client may well gain insight into the patterns of interaction and the different interpretations of the same event that are possible and which lead to situations of conflict. **Like changes in feeling, increased insight does not necessarily make things any different, but the additional knowledge may enable a client to tolerate higher levels of uncertainty** about a situation through which they are passing - for example, separation or bereavement.

(ii) *A Change of Feeling*

Having talked through an issue or dilemma, the client encounters deeper layers of feeling. This the counsellor acknowledges and helps encourage the client to release. Following such an **emotional discharge** or **catharsis**, the client recovers a greater degree of free attention or increased awareness of the room for manoeuvre within the situation.

Expression of feeling is often in contrast to a long-standing pattern of holding back, a feeling of pretending that "things will get better if only I hold myself together". Many clients need encouragement, or 'permission' to allow themselves to feel their feelings fully. This is often painful because it has built up over a long period. If a client is allowed to discharge old hurts freely (each time they surface) they recover greater freedom of action and autonomy to go on to make more effective and life enhancing decisions. Discharge of feelings is another preliminary for the client before they go on to changing parts of their world.

As a result of counselling, an individual's life circumstances may appear no different than before, but they may feel very differently about those circumstances. Much counselling is centred in this area of enabling the client to more freely express and 'own' their feelings, acknowledging their internal contradictions and thereby increasing their self acceptance. Such expressions of feeling may be important first steps in assisting clients to mobilise their energy toward doing something, but a change of feeling about something is a quite separate result from doing something about it.

(iii) *Making a Decision*

As a result of changing both their understanding (seeing things differently) and emotional release (feeling differently about the situation) a client can then move towards a readiness to make a new decision. This is a stage of **contemplation** and not action: a time of consideration of options and implications and deciding upon the **right course of action.** This is not the same thing as **taking action**. It may well take some time to work through this phase, and may well include trial - learning, rehearsal or further information gathering. At this stage however the client is working towards change and the focus is on the 'how' and not 'whether' to change or not.

Only when a decision is made does counselling move into activity outside the session. Over issues of concern and at times of crisis it is very often the case that the client becomes embroiled in a whole welter of competing demands and expectations which reduce an individual's power to initiate any decision. Counselling can help an individual to sort out the options, to assess their relative effect, and to consider their implications in a safe environment.

(iv) *Implementing a Decision*

It is **only when the client acts differently** and only when they do it out in the world **that counselling begins to make a difference to the client's day to day life**. Implementing decisions is often a very risky business. A lot is invested in a proposed change; fear of failure may produce crippling anxieties, sudden and unanticipated objections may begin to appear. The counsellor must be available to help the client choose the what, the how and the when and help them refine it to a **workable, achievable result.**

Once a decision is made, it remains to be put into effect. In short, **the client has to take responsibility for actually doing something**. Counselling can help the process by preparing the client for coping with its possible effects and for anticipating some of the likely blocks to success.

Counselling can stop at any point in this process but the counsellor needs to ask if the client's best interests are being served if they only gain insights, only discharge feelings or only ever contemplate change.

Becoming A Client

Many people find the admission that they may need the help of someone outside their personal network of support an admission of failure, somehow an indication that they are inadequate. Our society places a high value on people 'getting on' by themselves, and not needing help and looks upon activities like counselling as a service for social 'casualties'. Whilst this attitude prevails many people will put off seeking help for as long as they possibly can, often adding to their difficulties in the process. All too often they will seek to find reasons why they do not need it now, or that the four sessions they have had are 'enough'. This makes it all too easy for the client to discontinue counselling before the full benefits have been achieved.

Things To Attend To In Oneself

* If you are not interested in the client it will 'leak out' sooner or later. Appropriately pointing out a lack of interest in what the client is saying about their own life may be a step towards helping them understand why it is difficult for others to be interested. Being 'there' for the client includes pointing out how far you can remain engaged with what they have to say.

*   Equally if you are over-committed to the client's dilemmas, you will show it and it will get in the way of the client's freedom of action.

*   If you over-identify with the client you will be in danger of feeling what it is like for them all too well, and not being of much further use.

Chapter Twelve

Structuring Counselling:
Boundaries and Responsibilities

Counsellors have obligations to at least five sources: **themselves, their colleagues, their clients, their organisation**, and **their professional group.**

Counsellor and Client

It is important when counselling is taking place that the counsellor makes explicit, to themself at least, that this is what they are doing. This includes enabling the conditions to arise which promote open communication between client and counsellor. Also important is identifying any boundaries which may influence the amount of contact and time available to offer to the client.

The counsellor owes it to **the client**, who may be inexperienced in seeking help, to let them know something about 'what they are in for'. This may mean only a supportive comment, or it may mean outlining in some detail the methods the counsellor uses, the frequency of meetings, the expectations the counsellor has of the client for work outside the sessions and so on. In short, the counsellor is responsible for establishing the effective conditions for counselling to take place.

If the counsellor knows their role then they can help the client to learn theirs. Since most people are not 'natural' clients, they do have things to learn, and may have questions they are shy of asking. Attempting to ignore such issues by superficial displays of 'chattiness' can do much to prevent counselling reaching the quality of disclosure and challenge necessary to help the individual in difficulty.

The counsellor is responsible for making clear:

* Time - the length and frequency of sessions.
* Space - the location and provision of sufficient freedom from interference and distraction.

* Interventions - the range of ways of working with the client.
* Structure - overall clarity so that the client cannot misconstrue the situation or the reason for the meeting.

The purpose of counselling is the increase of personal responsibility in the client and/or the diminution of dependency. Clear guidelines given at the appropriate time can positively assist this process.

Boundaries

It is also the responsibility of the counsellor to be aware of boundaries within each helping relationship. There are certain issues and questions which need to be examined.

There are role boundaries, boundaries about confidentiality and boundaries that are about limits at which people are prepared to share, relate and act. Boundaries are about how I manage myself as a helper, how I know my limits and where my limits are.

* Who determines my limits?
* How do I respond as I approach my thresholds?
* What safeguards do I require?
* What do my boundaries help me avoid?
* How do my boundaries prevent relationships developing?
* What are the potentials for me becoming a rescuer or failing to help as a result of the boundaries I set?

Confidentiality

The more ambiguous the roles of the helper and the helped or the context of the meeting the more important it is to consider aspects of confidentiality, rather than to assume that it is understood in the same way by each of the two parties.

For a manager or member of staff, acting in the role of support and helper to a colleague, for example, there needs to be some clear understanding of the limits of the potential information that is being shared. Where the possibility exists for the helper to be able to make use of the information gained in a counselling session in other roles or in other settings, both must make clear how this is to be managed. It is not that such ambiguity should bring the enterprise to a halt, only that the trust that is required for the relationship to develop successfully is supported by clear 'contracts'.

It sometimes happens that the sheer weight of a problem pushes an individual into confiding to another who, in other circumstances they would think twice about, and this may cause unavoidable problems to both parties. When this happens it is better confronted sooner rather than later.

Where there is time for the helper and client to discuss their relationship and its boundaries the question of what information may go where and why, should be an essential aspect of the **contracting process.**

In informal helping arrangements, the issue of confidentiality can be overlooked until someone finds information that they thought was to be held has simply found its way into the social pool and feels understandably cheated. At other times, those with a management responsibility may feel themselves handicapped by having given a guarantee of confidentiality to a staff member who has then revealed information relating to their work performance that would need to be challenged.

Agencies and organisations may also have policies of their own about the limits of confidentiality and the appropriateness of who should offer a helping relationship to whom. That said however, there are many organisations that take for granted the role of the manager as a supervisor for the work of their own staff. Clearly, for staff in a helping role with others, the line manager is a most unsuitable and inappropriate figure from whom to receive supervision.

Confidentiality is one of the essential elements to establish at the outset of any helping relationship. With an increasingly impersonal society, individuals are rightly concerned whenever they speak to anyone in an official role, concerning what might happen to the information that they give. Individuals working in medical settings for example, need to be extremely clear about the range of information they seek and what they intend to do with it.

Contracts

The counsellor may work with formal contracts, i.e. with agreed and shared goals formulated by the client in an explicit way, or they may not. But the counsellor offers an implied contract of responsibility and dependability to his client. In addition, the counsellor has contracts with their organisation and professional colleagues.

The less explicit the contract is about what is offered and what is being attempted the more likely the help is to be unfocused.

In situations of open access, such as drop-in centres, there may be no clear contract and the helper can then be left feeling at the direction and mercy of the client, only able to respond on terms the client sets.

Contracting is a crucial skill for effective helping, especially in brief, short-term or crisis work. It enables the helper and client to prioritise their time effectively.

The Organisation

Organisations will place differing role expectations upon those they recognise in the helping role. Some of these will be explicit - like turning up on time, being in a certain place, operating within certain agreed boundaries, and so on; others will be much less so. **Role conflict** is inevitable for counsellors at some stage, though it does need to be kept to a minimum otherwise it can serve to discredit even the most positive work, or can be used by either side - counsellor or administration - as a way of avoiding dealing with important issues of practice which 'ultimately' have wider repercussions. Supervision or regular opportunities to consider such issues and to review practice in the light of changing circumstances is an essential requirement. Such regular exchanges of information help to minimise misunderstandings and to reduce the possibility for manipulative or mischievous clients creating unhealthy dramas that everyone is better without.

The Profession of Counselling

The helper in a counselling role has professional standards to uphold and promote. Association with others working in similar or related fields is not only an important source of mutual support and general professional development, but also an area in which to raise issues of concern and uncertainty that come to everyone involved in counselling. Standards of competence and consideration of ethical issues are a continuing feature of professional life, not matters to be sorted once and for all. Sometimes, too, a client brings forth an unexpected personal dilemma for the counsellor which requires the counsellor to call upon the skills of colleagues outside the situation.

Increasingly people involved in counselling are realising the importance of some form of peer support for themselves. This is reflected at the professional end of the helping continuum with considerable current discussion about the ethics of counselling and the accreditation of counsellors.

Chapter Thirteen

Working with Clients

The importance of early experience in the development of personality cannot be over-estimated. Such experience lays the foundations for the ways in which people interact in their wider world as they move through life. There is no space here to discuss this at any length, except to note its bearing upon the relationship that is to develop between the counsellor and the client. Though therapy is not being suggested here, what is important to realise is that clients in difficulty arrive with wide differences in the personal resources they can call upon to meet the challenges of their inner lives. How successfully or otherwise someone has coped with life changes in the past will affect how far and how freely they can respond to the one they are experiencing at the time they come for counselling.

Clients are always individual and their dilemmas are always unique. Nevertheless, three broad categories of client are worth noting. For convenience I am terming them the 'temporary' client, the 'problematic' client and the 'serious' client.

The Temporary Client

There are times in almost everyone's life when a crisis or problem emerges beyond our resources to deal with it effectively. Such individuals who come into counselling will usually have a personal history that has enabled them to establish effective and valuable relationships. They will have a measure of internal **personal security** (however much it may be off-balance at the moment) and a sense of **personal responsibility** for bringing about the changes they are seeking from counselling, and they will not have excessive illusions about the value of the counsellor or seek to foster an unrealistic dependence upon them. They will come to resolve a specific dilemma, will appreciate the help they get, and will leave the relationship once they have made the gains they are seeking. Often their difficulties will be focused upon inter-personal issues - specific crises to do with jobs, study and so on - or with enquiries into a particular dilemma they confront. Such clients are often those who offer the counsellor relatively early signs of change and development. The relationship is more nearly that of peers in which one party is temporarily drawing upon the resources of the other.

The Problematic Client

This second group of clients often enter into counselling for reasons similar to those above. Some current dilemma, an important relationship or a life crisis stimulates the search for help and assistance: a need to talk it through with someone outside the situation. But such clients differ from the temporary client described in the previous section, in that they have **much less in the way of personal resources** to enable them to overcome their current concern. **Their essential wholeness cannot be taken for granted.** There may be past experiences, not consciously recalled, which have significant influence upon how the individual relates to themself and others. There may be long-standing and underlying problems of moodiness and depression, for example, or a long history of repeatedly unhappy experiences in certain areas of life.

Involvement in counselling thus only begins to indicate a more serious state of affairs and a past history of incomplete or unhappy experiences. Sometimes the very relationships that counselling offers - the exclusive time and attention of another - is itself something which may complicate matters. Such care and attention can come to be seen as an expression of 'friendship' in its widest sense, leading to an expectation that the counsellor will somehow become involved in the life of the client and is someone available to the client as and when the need might arise. Initially such appreciation may be gratifying and, inadvertently, the counsellor can come to reinforce such false assumptions, taking a readier role in the life of the client than is either desirable or useful. Such 'boundary' problems then become a matter of concern, and lead to circular arguments about how the counsellor is failing the client. These have sufficient validity in them for the counsellor to feel unable to put them aside. The scene is set for poor helping of any kind.

Not all such clients end up attempting to engage their counsellors in this way. They are more likely to present **the counsellor** with a sense of almost hopeless expectation that nothing they attempt together will really change anything significantly. Being prepared to work with commitment when the client displays signs of passivity, reluctance or even hostility is a demanding role for any counsellor and the temptation to make comments or challenges that come from frustration and anger, rather than concern, are not always easy to avoid. It is just because these issues only emerge as contact increases that makes working with such clients so difficult. Often referral only gets thought of when the situation is practically uncontainable - a time long past when it can be most effective. Guilt, frustration and the sheer sense of impotence are not uncommon outcomes for counsellors dealing with such difficult clients.

The Serious Client

The serious client is the client most in need of help, for whom counselling will often change little in their lives, and who are often easiest to identify **These are people who for all manner of reasons are psychologically damaged**, who have aspects of their lives that are seriously impaired, or who function in certain situations with tortuous inadequacy. They will often come to counselling as part of an organisational response to attempt to enable them to integrate more successfully within the culture of the group to which they belong. Such clients have more serious difficulties than most counsellors can expect to cope with. What counsellors can do, however, is something which is far more constructive than inadequate psychic explorations, is to become a reliable source of safety and support - an anchor point for the individual to seek out at times of acute stress or challenge. Such long-term support can make all the difference to such individuals and **can help them to make progress with dignity and success through a placement or work experience that otherwise might simply collapse** from the unsympathetic and unskilled efforts of others who are unused to providing such a role. It is not always the case that individuals with serious difficulties **must** be moved on elsewhere by being referred to another agency. Often they can be very positively helped with the appropriate support and caring attention of specialist helpers on-site who are themselves in touch with appropriate referral agencies.

Chapter Fourteen

Types of Counselling

There are two principal types of counselling offered by most helpers: **remedial** counselling and **developmental** counselling. Most helpers see the need for working in a developmental way and not simply in a remedial capacity. But most organisations are unable and/or unwilling to release the resources required to introduce a developmental programme.

Remedial Counselling

Remedial counselling begins when an individual group or system experiences some difficulty. The time-scale is typically short-term, the theme is one of seriousness or crisis, and the request of the client is likely to be one of 'make this go away'. Suicide attempts, broken relationships, abrupt redundancy, are all examples of issues that require a remedial approach. The helper's role is usually seen as one of bringing things back to the familiar and reassuring pattern of the past before the crisis began. Sometimes a client will acknowledge that the crisis is part of an accumulating pattern, the latest in a series of similar events, and will seek to look beyond the alleviation of discomfort and begin to 'unscramble' the elements that contribute to the difficulty. 'Acute' stress is one of the times when most of us are prepared to take the necessary risk to do something to 'sort it out'. Chronic pain, however, is something most people learn to live with and accept. Only when there is some disturbance to the familiar pattern is there enough motivation to change.

It can be a source of frustration to many helpers that they could spend a majority of their time and effort in remedial counselling, in patching up emotional wounds and watching the individual return to a situation with nothing changed. It can be just as frustrating to give time, care and attention to someone in a crisis, only to realise that in three months time you will be doing exactly the same thing again, i.e. they will again be saying how much they now know about what's been happening and how it will not happen again. Usually they are right: they don't do it in the same way; instead they do it even more dramatically!

Acknowledging this is important for helpers if they are not to become demotivated and cynical. This is not to say that there are not many individuals for whom remedial counselling over a specific issue is not only appropriate but also successful.

Developmental Counselling

Most helping professions originally came into being for rehabilitative or remedial reasons. Guidance for schools students, for example, often came into being to help those students who for one reason or another failed to fit existing institutional arrangements and demands. "Even the oldest professions like teaching and the clergy, evolved out of a major desire to 'save' their subjects - in one case from stupidity, in the other from sin."

Our social world is characterised by the ever-increasing awareness of the rapidity of change. To **cope with change successfully requires flexibility, openness and the ability to let go of things left behind**. Patterns of work and leisure, sex-role expectations, etc. all challenge our traditional assumptions and are indicators that new patterns of demands are being made upon all of us.

Developmental counselling is based upon the assumption that individuals can develop and flourish when they are in healthy interaction with their surrounding world and not paralysed into passivity or reacting through fear. Developmental counselling assists that process of helping individuals increase their choices, enabling them to make use of their opportunities and take increasing responsibility for their actions and their consequences. An individual therefore does not have to be in a 'crisis' to benefit from the attention and careful listening of another. Developmental counselling can be seen as a strategy to enable things to continue to be fulfilling, and follows the maxim "You don't have to be sick to want to get better". An individual does not have to have poor relationships to want to improve on the skills they already possess for relating to others.

By preparing individuals for change through focusing on issues before they appear, developmental counselling can enable individuals to pass through a 'crisis' with greater ease, and can enable them to make fuller use of all the opportunities there may be, instead of becoming overladen with anxiety.

Much developmental counselling can be done through thematic groups. 'Life planning', 'decision-making' and 'weight control' are a few illustrations. Individual sessions may arise out of contact with a helper in order to overcome a crisis. Developmental counselling is an area of increasing growth.

Chapter Fifteen

Counselling Strategies

Defining The Outcome

The first and crucial step in resolving an issue is to **define** precisely and correctly **the desired outcome** the client is working toward. The counsellor's role is that of **clarifier** and **challenger**. Clarification is required to assist the client in assessing the realism of their desire. Challenge is frequently a necessary part of this process.

Often people define their outcomes negatively. They state what they want to stop happening: 'I don't want to get angry', 'I want to stop always being late'. **Negative outcomes are unsatisfactory** as aims for two principal reasons. Firstly, they give no clue as to what might need to happen instead, leaving the way open for other problems to come into being. Secondly, they do not acknowledge that the behaviour in question actually serves some purpose. Until a better way of serving this purpose, or a way of replacing it can be found, both counsellor and client can expect the behaviour to continue.

Defining the outcome positively in terms of 'I want...' enhances motivation and transferability of any learning, and helps to switch the **client's** attention into drawing behaviours and feelings from their situations, behaviours and feelings with which **they** wish to replace the negative pattern. Defining the outcome is not an easy process and is not something to work with in the early stages of a session, but it is something the counsellor needs to have in mind - that they are both there to **do** something.

Selecting Skills

The counsellor is responsible for identifying which skills will best enable them to help the client move towards the objective they have agreed together. It may be a question of helping the expression of blocked feeling, as in the case of loss; or of action planning, as in the case of deciding whether to apply for a new job.

Goal-Setting

Once the outcome has been defined, the skills, knowledge or behaviour required of the client to achieve it has to be considered. Not always will the counsellor share this information immediately with the client. However, the counsellor needs to consider the intermediate steps in the process: how to arrange the change process so that behaviours are 'in-step' with the client's increasing confidence, how to encourage attempts at rehearsal leading to trial efforts in the real situation, and how to enable the client to assess the consequences of such attempts both on themself and on others in a realistic way.

Consider the Constraints

A client lives within a network of surrounding lives. They live within a set of expectations and demands which are both limiting and supporting in their effects when it comes to change.

Clients may express a strong conviction about their wish to change, but find themselves handicapped by the network of relationships that they live amongst. The counsellor needs to pay attention to this issue and to help clients to clarify their understanding of the implications any change may have upon this network. It may be that expressing my irritation to my boss will enable me to feel better, but there may be other consequences that will follow.

Establish the Sequence

The counsellor is responsible for helping to identify the pattern and timing of the sequence of change with the client and for assisting in getting the process under way.

Monitoring

Over the sequence of meetings, an important feature is reviewing the results of any changes in the client's awareness or circumstances. Helping clients to appreciate the importance of monitoring their own behaviour encourages self-responsibility.

aviour
the
ver,
ow
he
al
to
n

in

out
ive
help
nay
oss
will

ing
the ... and for an office in whi... the

the
ling ... Helping
our

Section IV

The Counselling Process

Chapter Sixteen

Principles of Counselling

Counselling is based upon a belief in the fundamental impulse towards growth and maturity in individuals, and their capacity to take increased charge over their own lives. One view of the client's problem is to regard it as an attempt towards resolving that which has been unsuccessfully resolved in the past, this may mean that the client has to regress to earlier experiences and feelings to discover how the present conflict originates before they are able to move forward.

All behaviour is emotionally conditioned. It arises out of some experience (however distant) and is directed towards the future. However strange or bizarre, behaviour has meaning for the client.

Changes in behaviour result from changes in the emotional life of the client. To help bring about change it is necessary to understand the feelings which precipitate the behaviour.

Movement towards the resolution of conflict or an increase in effectiveness is only achieved when the client is involved in working out their own problems and defining their own solutions.

The counsellor offers the client time, space and skills to see the nature of their difficulties more clearly and to gain self-direction. Counsellors do not impose their own solutions, values, or judgements.

"The underlying common faith is the development of the relationship between the client and the therapist. It is through the strength and acceptance of the relationship that the client begins to achieve self-acceptance for those parts of themself which are difficult to acknowledge or integrate."

One definition of counselling: Counselling is offering a relationship to someone for the purposes of change. The relationship between counsellor and client is the medium of help.

Effective help rests on the capacity of the counsellor to establish a constructive relationship with the client.

To establish a constructive relationship with the client the counsellor must be responsive to the client in conflict.

The counsellor must accept responsibility for giving the interview (the particular form of the experience in relationship that counselling offers) both focus and direction.

The counsellor is responsible for employing effective skills and strategies to enable the client to develop.

It is important that the counsellor keeps their own conflicts and problems under control in the interview so that their own issues do not contaminate the client's work.

Permanent change in behaviour results from changes in the emotional life of the client.

To understand the behaviour or the conflict of the client and to help bring about change, it is necessary to understand the feelings that precipitated the behaviour or which lie behind the conflicts.

Understanding alone does not necessarily produce change.

The counsellor does not impose their own judgements, standards or solutions on the client.

The counsellor's own perspective is kept out of the way for the benefit of the client.

The counsellor respects and accepts the differences between the client and themself including such differences as sex, race, standards of behaviour, goals, social exceptions, values and religion.

The counsellor supports the strengths of the client.

The counsellor will leave the client free to use their own resources in testing solutions or making modifications to changes in the way they live.

The client has the resources within themselves to bring about change, however small.

Points to Remember

If you are genuine about making the client responsible for the content and disclosure in a session, then you must be prepared to take what comes.

Counsellors need to be careful not to project their own feelings on to the client, to interpret their behaviour too strongly, or to burden them with their own value judgements.

The 'here and now' is by and large the territory to get in and stay in.

Many clients may need support outside their session: if so, this needs thinking about.

Silences are important and useful.

Frequently feed back what you think you are hearing to check that you are both moving at the same pace.

Regular sessions help to make counselling part of life and not simply a crisis service.

What goes on in a session is not your property, it is that of your client, and you are not at liberty to use it in any way without their knowledge or consent. You are not on a fact-finding mission for any other agency.

'Presenting problems' are ways of testing out how far the relationship can take stress.

The temptation to give advice is the signal to resist it.

Be willing for problems to have untidy ends.

Don't be over-invested in your own interventions: be willing to let them go and to do something else instead.

Interpretations given too soon may confuse, or make understanding difficult, and make rejection more likely.

The degree of self-responsibility which counselling implies is not always easy for people to assume.

It is essential to remember the circumstances in which individuals have to act out their lives before making any suggestion.

Every problem is important to the person who has it and the solution novel to the person who tries it.

Chapter Seventeen

Problems for Those Seeking Help

To ask for and seek our help requires considerable courage on the part of most people, since our culture places high value on being competent, successful, achieving and so on, and to have to ask for help is often regarded, inaccurately, as the very opposite. Consequently, when a person first begins to notice an issue or problem arising, they push it away or refuse to think further about it in the fond hope that it will go away. When it does not and only grows worse for having been left unattended, it can become even harder to seek help, because the problem has become so big that it would only make the person appear foolish for not having come sooner. The prospective client is caught in their own double-bind. Heads they lose, tails you win.

Many people have the experience of seeking help only to have been met with insensitive handling, abrupt and inappropriate advice or having been patronised regarding their particular concern being any sort of problem in the first place. This kind of experience deters people from trying again.

Accepting Help

For the reasons given above, it may be difficult for an individual to accept help. Additionally they may have very strong beliefs and convictions which get in the way of accepting help. Those with beliefs about never asking other people for help or always relying upon your own efforts, find it extremely challenging to be open to help.

There are also certain kinds of life crises which have a potentially (and usually temporary) devastating effect upon the individual: examples are divorce, bereavement, and enforced redundancy. These can produce effects of such shock to the individual's self-esteem that having to ask for help, desperately needed though it is, is to place oneself in a position to invite further rejection.

Recognising The Need

It is often the case that those around us are the first to spot the signs that something is 'going on' and that we are not behaving in our usual ways. It is usually over issues that are personally felt that the individual concerned finds it most difficult to recognise or admit that a problem even exists, let alone that help might be required. Alcohol dependence can lead to alcoholism through the denial of the excessive drinker that they have any kind of problem at all. This kind of denial is not unusual.

It needs to be remembered that unless a person takes responsibility for the problem there is little that a helper can do. Sometimes people have to make very painful mistakes before they acknowledge that an issue exists which requires help to sort it out.

Behaviour Patterns

Most people associate change with difficulty, compulsion or even pain. They therefore not unnaturally dislike the idea of change, and will go to considerable lengths to avoid it. Also, well-established patterns of behaviour, or ways of relating to others developed over years of practice, have considerable investment attached to them. Changing such behaviours requires a great deal of commitment over a considerable period of time.

Accepting the Helper

It can sometimes be difficult to accept the helper, not only at the level of individual like or dislike, but because they represent all the competence, skills and ability that is presently absent in the client's own life. Clients sometimes go through a period of challenge in the worth of the helper's efforts, accusing the helper of not understanding their problem because 'You are too well-off, middle-class, young, old, etc.' or of seeking to establish an unrealistic relationship of dependence upon the helper.

Having to Trust

To get help requires trusting in the skill and expertise of another. At a time of vulnerability it means placing oneself in a position of extreme risk, laying the way open to exploitation. Such fears are genuine and should be handled sensitively.

Size of the Problem

The problem may seem too big, too small, too disgraceful, too pathetic, too complicated, or whatever, to seek out help or to accept it when it comes. Helping someone see that whatever the dimensions of the problem, something can be done to give a person greater choice over the options they have in front of them, is an important part of the helper's task.

Chapter Eighteen

The Counselling Process: An Overview

The strategies employed by the counsellor will depend upon the issue under review, the resources of the client, and - just as importantly - the amount of contact they have had. Attempting to define the outcome of counselling too early, for instance will only increase anxiety and perhaps lead to the client not fully expressing the complexity of a problem. As in any helping interview, a counselling session will follow a number of stages. The skills used at each stage will vary. There is usually an initial phase in which counsellor and client tentatively open the area of discussion before moving into the final action phase of deciding upon new steps to take as a result of new information, understanding or insight.

COUNSELLING: STAGES OF A SESSION

STAGE	PURPOSE	SKILLS
CONTACT	Establishing rapport Relationship-building	Listening Attending Matching Questioning
CONTRACT	Gaining commitment for change Establishing an initial outcome Establishing mutual responsibility Agreeing boundaries	Contracting

CLARIFICATION	Understanding the implications and effects of difficulties Enabling the individual gain greater understanding of their dilemma Identifying issues Listening for themes	Reflecting Paraphrasing Focusing Restating Prompting Summary
CHALLENGE	Identifying the impasse Identifying themes or patterns Supporting through discharge Re-contracting	Focusing Defining Confronting Immediacy Concreteness Specifying
CHOICE	Creating a climate of choice Helping move towards change Generating possibilities	Rehearsing 'Playing' Creativity
CHANGE	Enabling the individual to take charge Bring action into the world	Problem solving Goal-setting Action-planning Homework Revision
CLOSURE	Bringing the work and relationship to a close	Respect Genuineness Managing Endings

Chapter Nineteen

A Seven Stage Model of
A Counselling Session

The model offered here in detail has seven principal stages. Each stage has a central thrust or purpose for the counsellor and features the use of particular skills. This is not to say that the same skills, such as listening and attending are not important throughout - they are, but some skills will be likely to predominate at different times.

Stage 1: Contact and Relationship Building

Stage	Task	Skills
Contact	Relationship	Matching
		Mirroring
		Pacing
		Leading
		Listening
		Attending
		Questioning

Before any help can succeed, helper and client have to form an alliance to work together. It is primarily the helper's job to "model the process"; to indicate how the relationship will work, to indicate the boundaries and manage the efforts of both of them. This in itself can be a major task since some people have never had the experience of really being listened to or being given time and attention from someone else. It may cause embarrassment or anxiety to face the prospect of entering such an unfamiliar space. The helper can do much to put the client at ease by picking up cues from the client early and responding to them appropriately.

There are two principal tasks to accomplish in promoting effective contact:

* The removal of distractions and minimising of the potential for interruptions.

* The promotion of an atmosphere which will enhance the client's safety to disclose those things they need to talk about.

This raises the question of "where to begin"?

* If the helper spends too long relating to the client this may be a way of never getting round to the crucial material. Lots of good chat may happen, but nothing much may change.

* If the helper begins with too abrupt a request to get to the heart of things, the client is likely to back off and freeze up.

Much that the helper can do at this stage can be undertaken at the non-verbal level by:

* Sitting in an open, expectant but not threatening way.

* Holding an open gaze, rather than a stare.

* Inviting the client to choose where to begin.

* Mirroring the client's overall body posture.

* Matching the client's language and using their preferred channels of communication.

* Pacing the client's world-view in an attempt to understand their **frame of reference** rather than challenging their ideas and beliefs too early.

Once the client begins to feel you are interested enough in understanding how it really is for them and are taking the trouble to learn about their individual **model of the world**, they will be more willing to let you **lead** them into new areas of exploration and clarification - the next stage of helping.

Rapport

Possession of the skills and qualities inherent in creating the core conditions and an understanding of what the client is saying is not enough. It is vitally important to communicate such understanding effectively. It is possible to improve the skills of communicating such qualities with training, but no amount of training will create what is basically not there.

Rapport is clearly an essential element in the early stages of the formation of a working alliance between counsellor and client. Successful rapport depends upon two important considerations with regard to the willingness of the counsellor to:

* Begin their conversation at a suitable place that is near the major purpose of their meeting i.e. somewhere close to the topic at hand.

* Move at a pace that does not upset or put the client off thereby making it more difficult for them to respond well.

Rapport is about establishing an effective relationship, one suitable for the purpose, in that sense those involved do not have to like each other but they do have to create sufficient confidence and trust that they can accomplish their work together.

The helper's role is crucial in setting the tone and in creating the context for the client to respond.

Any helping activity has to begin somewhere, but if you do not know the client well there is a danger in starting too close to the subject matter and increasing the client's anxieties. However, if you begin too far from the topic, there is every danger of never getting to it at all, or only when the time available is running out.

Rapport can be thought as having five elements:-

* **Willingness** - a genuine interest in accomplishing a result.

* **Freedom from distractions** - the ability to give your full attention to the task in hand.

* **Joining and leading the subject** - the ability to **match** the client's language, **mirror** the client's behaviour and **pace** their belief system, before moving anywhere else.

* **Remembering what you are doing** - being flexible enough to respond to the client rather than expecting the client to adapt to you.

* **Acuity** - having sufficient awareness to both detect and understand the signals the client gives and the responses that they make.

The central purpose of establishing rapport is to generate in the client a sense of being understood whilst you are able to gather information central to the task that you are there to accomplish.

Rapport can be considered as having four levels:

* There is rapport at the **content level.** You generate for the client a sense of their being understood, by being able to relay back to them what they have said.

* The second is at the level of **feeling.** You can convey to the client a sense of your understanding of what it is that they feel about what they are saying.

The third and fourth levels of rapport are more complex and difficult. However, if you can confidently create rapport in depth, the work that you can do with the client will have consequent benefits.

* The third level of rapport can be called **advanced empathy.** This means being able to take what the client has said and to be able to draw attention to what has not been described but which is also meant. It is akin to filling in the spaces between the words. If done sensitively the client not only feels understood, but also understood in a way that they themselves are groping to discover.

* The fourth level of rapport might be called **projective empathy.** Here the client is not only understood, but the counsellor can so closely identify the **frame of reference** the client is using that they can give other situations which are congruent to the client's world view. The effect is to help the client realise that someone else can understand even that which they are not yet able to express confidently.

Levels of Understanding

There are three levels of understanding which are progressively more effective. Being aware of these levels enhances the helper's understanding of their level of engagement within the helping relationship.

* understanding about you – this is the level of understanding the client through someone else's perceptions. Helpers often have this level following a referral from another practitioner or carer. This is remote understanding.

* Understanding you – this is the level of understanding someone through the helper's own perceptions. It is based upon the helper's feeling, knowledge, skills, or – in other words – the helper's own internal frame of reference.

* Understanding with you – this is the level that is most demanding and the one required for developing effective rapport. It requires us to aside everything but our common humanity and see the world as the client sees it – in doing so we enter into their reality without becoming lost in it.

Stage 2: Contracting

Stage	Task	Skills
Contract	Gaining commitment for change	Reflecting
		Paraphrasing
	Establishing an initial outcome	Focusing
		Restating
	Establishing mutual understanding	Prompting
		Summary
	Agreeing boundaries	

The stages of contact and contract are often closely linked in time, with the helper building the relationship through the discussion and exploration of what the client hopes for from the helper and the relationship.

It is important to recognise that the counsellor is responsible for making clear:

* **Time**   the length and frequency of sessions

* **Space**   the location and providing sufficient freedom from interference and distraction

* **Interventions**   the range of ways of working with the client

* **Structures**   overall clarity so that the client cannot misconstrue the situation or the reason for the meeting

Having set the counsellor's boundries for the client, which may range from a supportive comment to a more detailed addressing of the above issues, then the scene is set for the client and helper to focus on the client's needs. The concept of establishing a mutually agreed contract with the client is based on a number of underlying philosophical assumptions:

* a person has the ability to change

* a person can take responsibility for their own destiny

* a person can work collaboratively

* a person has the ability to fulfil their own potential

Within this stage there are a number of questions which will help both the client and the helper to reach a mutually agreed contract. The following are not exhaustive, although they are perhaps the minimum.

1. **What do you want . . . what do you really want?**

   A contract goal needs to be phrased in a positive way – i.e. I want to spend more time reading; negative goals – i.e. I want to stop wasting my time; rarely result in long term change, as the very process of working on negative phrases reinforces the negative state. Much of the work in the counselling relationship is related to helping the client find something they really want and that is worth working towards.

   In Transactional Analysis (T.A.) terms, this question is aimed to discover where the energy of the client is in regard to change – asking the Child – if the motivation for change is external to the client – i.e. someone else wanting the client to change – then the outcome of the work is unlikely to result in any long term change.

2. **Is it realistic?**

   This is an Adult check (T.A.). Has at least one other person achieved this in the world? It is impossible to 'make' someone else change – third party counselling is rarely successful. Given your present circumstances and network is the change possible?

3. **How will you and I know when you have achieved the change?**

   If the goal is too general it will be difficult to tell if the client has achieved it, and they may be 'working on it' for eternity. The more the person has a *detailed* perceptual sense of how it will be when the change has occurred the more useful (i.e. positive visualisation/sensualisation):

   what will you be doing

   how will you feel?

   who will notice? (with names and detail)

what thoughts will you have?

how will others see you?

what will you sound like? etc.

The change needs to be specific and reportable, demonstrable or observable.

4. **What will you have to give or give up to get it?**

    All change has a 'price'. It may be in terms of facing a fear, or a sense of power or powerlessness, money, endings, time, commitment, loss or turmoil. It may be that the client decides that having explored and stated the goal, confirmed it is possible, outlined clearly how they would know a change has occurred, they decide it is not worth the price . . . yet . . . or maybe ever. The counselling relationship may end at this point. If it doesn't then the next question is . . .

5. **What is the first step and by when?**

    This aims to help the client to begin to change from the start. It checks the level of commitment to change i.e. if the client is ready to take on the challenge of change **now.** It builds the beginning of an action plan and enables the next phase to either build on the success, or to explore how come the first step was not achieved.

    It may be within this area, that the client outlines who might support them in their change i.e. helping forces.

6. **How might you sabotage yourself?**

    This question focuses the client on past behaviour and how they get in their own way. This is often in the form of internal messages. The helper is exploring with the client self-defeating instructions, which may have been very helpful at one time, but now are old patterns that get in the way of the grown-up situation. In T.A. terms the question examines if the agreed goals are a working alliance of the Adult with co-operation from the Free Child, rather than from Adaptive Child.

Bringing the potential sabotages into the open will help to reduce their influence. Specific work may be done on how to reduce these influences further.

Another part of this question relates to the helper – are you helping to sabotage the client by not helping them to be specific and detailed, not challenging them on what seem to be incongruities, or on the way they seem to be getting in their own way even in the contracting phase. Letting a client leave the session, with the helper thinking 'they'll never do it' and not voicing it, is a method of sabotage and of assisting the client to re-live their old patterns.

Initially the contract will often be loose and informal and only through further development will it become more specific and clearer to the client and helper. The contract need not be too detailed or too rigid. It needs to offer structure for the relationship and the work to be progressed without scaring or overwhelming the client. Therefore the contracting stage is not a one off event and will be re-visited in the form of review, revision, focus and evaluation throughout the counselling or helping relationship, and so avoiding inflexibility and irrevocable commitment to whatever the initial goals were.

If the helper and client do not know where they are going, they will always end up somewhere, it must be that it isn't a place worth visiting. If we agree where we are going and get somewhere else we will learn a lot! It is important to have a sense throughout the work that the map drawn at the outset is not necessarily the territory, and through the stages of the helping relationship, walking the territory may well result in changes to the map being made. The changes are best made explicit, rather than being implicit. Often the individual's issues are based on living out implicit contracts that would be usefully made explicit. The whole process of contracting provides a good model for reviewing implicit contracts in the 'outside' world.

The context defines the contract

The contexts that will need to be taken into account to reach a realistic outcome are:

Client – Internal (internal world the client lives in)
External (the world they live in, expectations, external boundaries)

Counsellor – Internal
External (the organisational boundaries, role boundaries etc)

As a helper I need to be aware of my own and the client's external situation and internal world.

Stage 3: Clarifying - Getting the Story

The third stage of a counselling relationship is to help clarify the concerns the client is attempting to express.

Stage	Task	Skills
	Offering permission	Open Questions
	Identifying Issues	Reflecting
Clarify	Listening for Themes	Restating
	Testing understanding	Paraphrase
	Identifying the impasse	Summary

Someone in difficulty may well seek only an immediate solution to the problem. Nevertheless the issue still presents them with an opportunity to take a further step in their life journey.

It is useful at this stage to remember that clients need their problems, and since they have usually taken a long time to get them, and have spent a while hanging on to them before asking you for help then you can remember that it will do them no great harm to keep the problem until they come up with **their own solution.** This should be sufficient for you to resist all efforts to provide 'solutions'. If the problem or the crisis really were that easy to solve why do you suppose they are so 'stuck'?

Resist helping the client in favour of **gathering a full description** of the problem they experience. It can be tempting to believe that you know the client's problem at this early stage. Yet you cannot possibly know how it is for them even when they tell you. If you are reasonably sure you know what is going on, it will do no harm to keep it for later when the client may well be able to use it. This stage of counselling is focused around helping the client gain **coherence in their account of themselves.** The helpers task is to facilitate that process and gather a sense of how the client comes to have the difficulty they face at this particular time. As the story unfolds the counsellor will be alert to listen for any 'blind spots' the client has overlooked, any **unexamined assumptions** they are making about themselves, others, the situation or the world in which they live, which are **limiting their freedom of action.**

It is important to be free to listen to the story as it unfolds and if you are not distracted then you have time to think of how to respond and where to go next.

Stories have both a content, a sequence of events and a meaning or feeling **tone**. The importance of the story lies in the sense of meaning the client has or has not got in what has been happening to them.

Some stories are: complex;
some are only discovered in the telling;
some deepen as they unfold;
and some reveal many possible directions.

Points to remember

*   The story may turn out not to be the story.

*   What does it mean for this person to carry this issue in their lives?

*   How does the person feel about what is happening to themself and about themself from inside their circumstances?

*   Some people may show little initial commitment to telling their story.

*   The client may believe telling their story won't change anything (and, of course, strictly speaking they are right).

*   The story may be deeply moving and the client may need considerable reassurance.

*   It is a risk to raise the lid on yourself or to dig your own pit and them jump in.

*   Sometimes telling the story is sufficient for the person to gain either insight or understanding about their difficulty.

*   Sometimes it is enough just to share the difficulty knowing it is yet no nearer to resolution.

*   Most often telling the story seems to remind the client of how far the situation has developed and how much there may be to do before any change is likely.

Stage 4: Challenge

Stage	Task	Skills
Challenge	Selecting themes	Focusing
	Challenging implications	Defining
	Support through	Specifying
	discharge	Immediacy
	Re-contracting	Concreteness
		Immediacy

Following clarification of the issue or difficulty, which helps the client reveal to themself something of the understanding they have of their dilemma, the sessions have to move forward. In the clarifying stage the control over what happens next rests very much with the client. They can decide how far to go, just what they disclose and how they tell their story. Once a session moves on from examining the implications of the situations described then the control and influence transfers across to the counsellor who will ask questions that push and challenge the client. This can be done with sensitivity and skill to the point where the client barely notices it, or it can be a very direct, confronting experience. However it needs to be done with the client's interests paramount and not the need of the counsellor to demonstrate how well they know what the client has overlooked. This is not counselling 'to make sure they have got the right message'.

This is the stage of:

*   Looking for the pattern underlying the story

*   Working with feelings at a deeper level

*   Recognising the client's ownership of the issue

*   Discovering the impasse caused by rigidity in behaviour or fixed belief

*   Identifying unused resources, unnoticed opportunities and hidden potentialities

If the client is to move forward something has to give way; boundaries may have to be challenged; action may be necessary. This is where the identification of unused resources and capitalising on unnoticed opportunities or hidden potential becomes crucial.

All this involves risk and uncertainty and the consequences for self-image and self-esteem are likely to be high. The question for the helper is 'can the counsellor and client evaluate the issue so as to make the uncertainty manageable?'

For a challenge to succeed it is essential that the client 'owns' the issue i.e. takes responsibility for their part in whatever situation they are in. Finding ways to displace the problem away from oneself, to make-up excuses why they can't change or to play games with themself in the hope that the problem will go away all have to be surrendered if the client is to move forward. Energy spent avoiding the issue is energy needed to resolve the dilemma.

In all this the client needs to feel supported by the counsellor. This is the phase of 'tough loving' where attempts to 'rescue' the client from the potential painful realisations they may face will only delay the inevitable; where false reassurance is more likely to be an attempt at protecting the counsellor themself.

In the end we have to exchange blame (upon others) for pain (of realisation) and a counsellor who must keep things 'nice' will help no-one, not even themselves: just as a counsellor interested merely in pushing the client into seeing what they need to do will only be counterproductive. If the client pushes themselves prematurely or does it to please you, where is the real learning? Often such premature efforts backfire and the client is left more demoralised than ever.

The challenge stage requires a **balance between love and power** on the part of the counsellor, a sufficient degree of compassion to be present for the client rather than to see them 'get better', 'make a go of it' or any of the other rationalisations we might put forward and enough power to hold the challenge effectively when the client's frightened, inner child wants to run away to the safety of keeping things the way they have always been. Any anxiety or uncertainty on the part of the counsellor will only get in the way of offering a clear non-defensive challenge. Unsolicited challenge, it is worth remembering, is hardly ever successful and that is why it is worth waiting until this point in a session to offer a challenge, when the relationship can bear the weight of the confrontation of the client with themself.

Sometimes the conflict the client is struggling with lies not in the world, in a relationship or situation they wish to act differently toward, but often the conflict is an internal opposition between competing values, for instance the need for security versus the risk of trying something new.

Many internal conflicts have an **exaggerated** dimension to them: either an exaggerated need for something, approval, recognition, or perfection for instance; or the pursuit of **the one right way** which will make everything alright again; or an exaggerated fear of being rejected, condemned or that some ultimate catastrophe will ensue.

These exaggerated concerns may have led in the past to the client repeatedly using self-defeating behaviour that only reinforces the very pattern they want to change, or may have only seemed to set up evasions and avoidance behaviour.

Working with Challenge

Always allow the client the opportunity to challenge themselves, to discern the discrepancies and incongruences in their account of themselves for themselves. **Self challenge is the most potent form of challenge.** It allows the client the opportunity to assume responsibility for taking themselves through this stage. That way they can take all the credit for themselves.

It is important to challenge the **right** issue. By right we mean the one the client is most ready to respond to effectively, not right as in what you think is most important or what you think the client should tackle. Sometimes the issue you both identify turns out not to be **the** issue and the client has to return to a further stage of clarification. This will only be able to occur if you are steady in holding the first challenge so the client has an opportunity to know where they are in relation to themselves and the issue. It is therefore important not to be side-tracked by following up irrelevant issues or smoke-screens, including exaggerated emotional responses.

Before any challenge can succeed the counsellor and client need to gain **as complete a representation as possible of the internal experience** the client goes through at the time the problem occurs by using **focused questions.** If possible get the client to bring the problem into the room to demonstrate just how they look or what tone of voice they actually use. This will show you where and how they get stuck and you will not have to rely solely on their description. Counsellors need to be imaginative in finding ways to accomplish this.

Whilst the manner of the challenge the counsellor offers needs to be tentative and tactful and should look to identify examples that identify the client's potential to work with an issue, it is also important for the counsellor to have had experience of being challenged themselves. Openness to challenge oneself offers a valuable role model to the client. The counsellor should remember that **there must be sufficient rapport** for the challenge to hold, you have to be both interested and care enough and that your challenge should be open to being refused: "I'm not ready to deal with that yet," or even rejected: "I think you got it wrong." If you are really there for the client you can always return to the subject at another time. Remember to remain positive in the challenge and not to become over-invested in any result.

Areas of Challenge

There is a whole series of polarities which many issues become reduced to. These are frequently related to self-limiting beliefs about one's own talent or potential or oneself, about moral constraints or fixed ideas about personal identity. Beneath the impasse you will often find one or all of the following issues at work, a sense of **hopelessness** (as in "I couldn't possibly do that") or a sense of **helplessness** (as in "People like me shouldn't expect any more or don't have any right to...") or **worthlessness** ("I am just not worth anybody's trouble to put this right. It doesn't really matter anyway.") Helping shift such deep stated beliefs is not easy and a **modest** improvement is the aim.

Other conflicts can often be identified as a struggle between:

What I ought to do	v	What I want to do
What I think	v	What I feel
What I say	v	What I end up doing
What I want for myself	v	What others expect of me
What I think of myself	v	What I'd like to aspire to

Other conflicts are focused at the level of a conflict of two sorts of values i.e. security versus opportunity.

There can be an exaggerated need for:
* approval
* recognition
* perfection
* being right
* pursuing something that the client believes will change everything

An exaggerated fear of:
* rejection
* condemnation
* sense of failing
* catastrophe

Which may have led in the past to:
* repeatedly using self-defeating behaviour that reinforces the cycle
* evasion and avoidance
* smoke-screening the real issues
* playing games
* displacing responsibility and blaming others

The Manner of the Challenge

*	Be tentative	"It's my impression that..."
*	Be tactful	"I've got a sense that..."
*	Build upon success	"When did you last achieve this or anything like it?"
*	Be concrete and specific	"You have said how much you care, but each time, I have noticed your hand hitting your wrist."
		"Are you sure you know how you feel?"
*	Relate it to aspects the client can undertake	"What time could you find to work this out?"
		"How much do you think you will have to give?"
*	Challenge strengths to develop rather than point out failings.	

Challenge Questions

> What is the pay-off for things being like this?
> What have you already tried?
> What happened?
> What would happen if you did...?
> What is the worst thing that could happen?
> What would you really like to do?
> What stops you?
> Who says you can / cannot?
> How do you know?
> How do you feel about...?

Movement is challenge. Challenge is designed to assist the client to move forward, to liberate their own inner resources, skill and potential. The counsellor needs to look for **points of leverage** to alert the client to qualities they already possess but which they could exploit more successfully in their own lives.

Challenge is offered to:

* open a new perspective
* increase awareness
* widen options
* discharge feelings

Challenging Implications

Stage	Tasks	Skills
Challenge	Selecting themes	Focusing
	Challenging implications	Defining
	Support through discharge	Specifying
	Identifying options	Concreteness
		Immediacy
		Challenge

Counter-productive Challenge

There is a series of interventions that can occur any time in a counselling session and which are likely to hinder the client. In themselves they are often experienced as challenging in a threatening rather than productive way. They rarely help. Amongst the most frequent are:

Commanding:	ordering or directing the client to change however benignly expressed.
Warning:	pointing out, however gently, the unpleasant consequences of continuing as they are.
Moralising:	offering, however rationally, your own position as the one to adopt.
Advising:	offering a solution of your own to the client's supposed problem.
Lecturing:	using logically convincing explanations that are supposed to show the client the way.
Ridiculing:	belittling the client's best efforts to help themselves.
Interrogating:	questioning the client to help them face up to what you know they are avoiding.
Humouring:	distracting yourself and the client into letting yourselves off the hook.
Reassuring:	sympathising or consoling the client is not what you are there for.
Approving:	agreeing with the client is irrelevant to the task.

Challenge and Irrational Beliefs

Many of the impasses that we experience in our lives are concerned with the influence of irrationally held beliefs. We become, for example, caught in a struggle between two competing choices: we cannot seek the solution to a problem by asking for what we want without feeling guilt in ourselves or thinking we will appear selfish in the eyes of others. Some of the characteristics of such beliefs are set out below:

Demanding: they often include elements of "must", "should" or "ought".

Self-fulfilling: because we have always failed in the past we expect to in the future and we make sure we do - all without realising it.

Self-evaluating: they are highly judgmental of self - the opposite of self-forgiving and self-accepting.

Awfulness: there is usually a sense of heightened emotionality or crisis about events.

Misattribution: there are elements of the situation that claim exaggerated importance, and responsibility is shifted onto self or others or away from self or others in unrealistic ways.

Repetition: we indoctrinate ourselves with other related self-defeating ideas so they assume an often unquestioned consistency.

Five Steps to Challenge the Consequences of Irrational Beliefs

These steps are drawn from the work of Albert Ellis, the founder of Rational Emotive Therapy (RET)

A: There is an activating event.

B: This triggers the irrational belief that determines what the event **must** mean.

C: There are a set of predictable consequences that follow: a pay-off.

D: To change the pattern, there must be a successful challenge or **dispute** of the irrational belief.

E: Leading to a successful effect.

Stage 5: Choice

Stage	Tasks	Skills
Choice	Creating a climate of choice	Rehearsing
	Helping move towards change	'Playing'
	Generating possibilities	Creativity

Whereas in the challenge stage, control passed from client to counsellor it now returns to the client. Following a successful challenge, there is a sense of renewed enthusiasm, a willingness to go forward and a more committed potential for change. However, the freeing of energy and the increase of insight needs to be managed so that the client moves forward at a pace and in a way that they can successfully maintain. Over-eagerness at this stage can throw the client into making ill-considered plans and taking hasty action that may be a *'sabotage'* that undermines the hard work that it has taken to get this far.

The **choice stage** enables the helper and the client work together to take stock of options, consider courses of action and 'play' with possibilities. One choice is no choice; two choices only adds up to a dilemma, *real choice begins with three options.* Helping the client to generate the *'true third alternative'* – the direction that offers a greater sense of freedom and responsibility is the essence of the choice stage.

Where the original dilemma may have been expressed as a forced choice conflict: e.g. 'I feel like I want to do this, but I know I should do that' following the challenge stage, the client will have more awareness to see beyond the imprisoning restrictions of the two choices. There may be many possibilities now. This itself may cause a new problem; 'How do I choose when I have so many options before me?' So often in a counselling relationship, the client comes face to face with the realisation that it is not that the world does not offer them the potential to choose what would most suit their best interests, but that they lack any skilled practice in knowing how to choose wisely. Generating ideas, rehearsing possibilities and assessing the 'likely' consequences can be a valuable learning stage in the overall progress of the client. From such activities the client may begin to recognise new elements that require consideration, or to evaluate the potential effects of a planned change that may lead to a further stage of clarification – not of the original dilemma, but of the impact of the proposed change upon their network or their life circumstances.

For some clients it was better when they had no choice, because then they didn't have to take the responsibility that this stage inevitably requires.

The choice stage is akin to the earlier clarification stage, but with an added dynamism. It is a time for clarifying the options, generating the possibilities and weighing alternatives in a way that is free of consequences. That is why it can be seen as a 'play' time for both helper and client. Work avoided at this stage can cost dearly later, when the client discovers that implications that could have been anticipated have simply been ignored. No-one needs to practice their mistakes! Good work at this stage can leave the client with a richer sense of their own capabilities and resources for taking action and becoming more effective in the world. This is the next step.

Stage 6: Change

Stage	Tasks	Skills
Change	Enabling the individual to take charge Bring action into the world	Problem solving Goal setting Action Planning Homework Revision

Change comes about through choice

Personal problem solving is taken up at a later stage in the manual and much of what could be said here is raised there. For the counsellor however, it is important to remember that nothing changes in the client's life until they begin to act. It is not sufficient to have an insight or come to a decision for change to take place. It has to be implemented. And at this stage the client may well become nervous and anxious all over again at the prospect of what they now know they have committed themselves to. Since practising mistakes and attempting things that fail have no place in counselling, the client and counsellor together have to build a model of action that has **manageable chunks of activity and realistic steps** that the client can with a reasonable degree of confidence expect to accomplish and report back upon.

Reviewing what actually happened in the light of experience is an additional and important source of further learning that the client might overlook but the counsellor should not. Similarly accepting a statement such as "Oh yes it went fine", and not probing what took place actually fails the client. There is everything to learn from a success so that the client can identify those skills and behaviours and then can draw upon them next time. Such exploration begins to generate positive behaviour in the client and help move away from a purely remedial style of working.

Stage 7: Closure

Finally the client has to say goodbye. What they came to learn they now know and the time has come for them to move on even from you. This is not an easy stage to manage or do well. Both parties are likely to have a good deal invested in the work they have done together and the relationship that has grown. A good counselling relationship can become a messy one because the counsellor cannot find a 'good time' to broach the ending or the client 'Isn't sure if they are ready to leave you'. Talking about endings a long time before they are likely can help to prepare both people beforehand.

Closure is about completion, of the work, or the issue. A time to look back and make sure what the client is taking away, of the journey they have made. It is an opportunity for the counsellor to help by pointing out landmarks they too have noticed and offering appropriate disclosures about the meaning the work has had for them too. It is about being real; and partings can be moving. There is no need to pretend you are unaffected in order to make it "easy" for the client.

Stage	Tasks	Skills
Closure	Ending the work Closing the relationship Evaluating the time spent together	Respect Empathy Genuineness Authenticity

Chapter Twenty

Counselling Skills

A Counselling Skills Framework

John Heron (1986) devised a very useful framework for examining the skills involved in helping situations which can be applied to counselling. The system of **'Six Category Intervention Analysis'** looks at inter-personal interaction as fitting into six broad categories. Each has its own strengths and limitations.

The Six Category System

Different counsellors possess different degrees of skill in different areas. They also have preferred strategies for the various stages of a session. For example, some counsellors are very effective in confronting their clients in a supportive and non-threatening way; others find that they feel they handle such situations less well. Training in the use of counselling skills helps counsellors to identify the areas in which they work well and those which are open to further development. There is no 'ideal' profile of a counsellor. It is much more important to be aware of the strengths and limitations of your own individual style.

Prescriptive: Advice-giving, telling, authoritative intervention offering, large-scale interpretations.

Appropriately used this can help bring about major insight or understanding. If the client is in severe difficulties, giving strong prescriptions can be a caring and responsible form of protecting the client (from suicide, for example), **but** large-scale interpretations can easily be used to demonstrate the skills of the counsellor at the expense of **the client** working things out for **themself.** It is open to the counsellor taking over the client's problem. Clients can become demoralised by all you know about them which they don't understand about themselves.

Informative: Offering new facts and information, interpreting behaviour.

Less authoritative than prescriptive interventions, informative ones offer the client a more immediate interpretation of the current situation. They can usefully serve to move the client forward to new understanding, by helping to fit pieces of the jigsaw together, but informative interventions can remove important learning from the client. The temptation to appear the wise leader has to be recognised.

Confrontive: Challenging restrictive thinking, beliefs, attitudes and behaviour.

Challenging a client in the safety of a session can help to focus on the unanticipated consequences of intended actions. For many of us, there are some areas of conflict between what we would like to do and what we feel we ought to do, and counselling often needs to work in this area. **But** many people, both counsellors and clients, find confrontive interventions potentially threatening and avoid them. Because it is challenging, over-use of confrontive interventions can lead the client to switch-off and not hear.

Facilitative Interventions

Catalytic: Eliciting self-direction, assisting the individual to enquire within, and reflecting back the content and feeling of client responses. Enabling full expression of distress can bring about a recovery of attention to problem-solving.

Encouraging openness to feeling positive as well as negative is an important resource for full living. **But** many clients are 'blocked' from expressing certain feelings. Often such feelings are withheld because of personal myths about potential consequences. "If I cry it might never stop," or "Men should always cope," or "Feelings don't change anything [so I'll stay miserable]," are common examples. If clients work with feelings which the counsellor has not looked at and experienced for themself, and the counsellor cannot handle them, the client will sense this, with messy results.

Cathartic: Working with the feelings of the client.

Enabling discharge of painful feelings or memories. Offering permission to release repressed anxieties to provide 'free attention' to work more productively, but allowing and encouraging feelings can be a great challenge to some clients.

Supportive: Being with the client, offering non-judgemental appreciation and positive affirmation of worth.

Bringing clients into a fuller appreciation of themselves is a central part of counselling. Assisting clients to a recognition of what they can do for themselves and have already done can be a positive force in dealing with the current dilemma. **But** support that is qualified or partial is damaging, as in "Don't worry about it, we all have to go through..." thus diminishing the individual's difficulties. Support means being there and seeing it out.

Through the use of the six categories, counsellors can identify a profile of their favoured and most troublesome or avoided areas of activity, and begin the process of practising these skills so as to develop greater flexibility over the whole range. Where individuals are restricted in their freedom of expression, the use of paced exercises can help to broaden the resources available to a client.

Clarifying Skills

Many of the skills used during the **exploratory** stage of a session are those which help the client clarify or enlarge their ideas, thoughts or feelings further. They are designed to elicit **self-direction** in the client. These types of intervention aim to broaden the shared information between counsellor and client:

* To help clarify the issue under review.
* To explore an aspect further.
* To examine the implications of the way things are.
* To consider alternative strategies.
* To increase choice, understanding and self-direction.

Open Questions:

"Tell me more, please."   "Why?"   "How?"
"When, specifically does this happen?"
"What else do you notice that's different?"
"What are you aware of?"

Client-centred Questions:

All questions which seek information about the external or internal world of the client.

Selective Reflections:

Taking a part of a statement from within a longer speech and selectively reflecting the phrase or image back either with similar tone and intonation or with tone and intonation deliberately exaggerated.

Reflecting:

Playing back in full a complete statement to the client in order to enable them to hear it and measure its effect.

Client: "I really hate my father."
Counsellor: "You really hate your father."

Repetition:

Asking the client to repeat a statement, phrase or word exactly in the manner they have just expressed it. (Sometimes asking to repeat it with an opposite intonation).

Client: "I wind myself up before every exam - do I do it myself? I'd never thought of it that way."

Summary:

The counsellor summarises the main points from within a series of statements and provides the client with an opportunity to confirm, deny or change the counsellor's understanding.

Counsellor: "Let me see if I'm sure I've heard what you're saying..."

Testing Understanding:

Deliberate requests to summarise and test out if the counsellor has indeed got the essence of the story or scene. Frequently clients discover what they mean as they talk. Such checks for understanding are therefore useful to both parties.

Empathic Building:

Elaborations of the client's meaning which enable both client and counsellor to investigate the **possible** implications of suggestions. Such elaborations are offered non-possessively and are made to aid the client, not to suggest the counsellor's depth of insight.

Use of Self-disclosure:

The counsellor's use of appropriate self-disclosure, sharing a feeling, an experience or an observation from within their own life, can bring about a helpful release or further work in the same area by the client. To know that someone else has experienced similar events in similar ways can be a great relief and can help the client to accept what is happening in themself.

Challenging Skills

The confrontive dimension moves all the way along the spectrum from mild requests to reconsider the weight of a statement and its appropriateness to the context, (e.g. "Can you describe what you mean when you say you feel angry?") to much more challenging interventions that confront the individual with aspects of thinking, attitude or behaviour which are severely limiting their action. **Confrontive interventions are in**

the realm of feedback, where the counsellor is in the position of an external monitor to the client, able to make helpful comments and suggestions as a result of what they see.

Many people have little clear idea about how their behaviour is seen by other people, and therefore, have little accurate information about its effects on others. The deliberate request for feedback from other people seems an invitation to others to become negative and judgmental. Once we know how our behaviour is being interpreted, we might then decide to change. But before any change is possible, we require **accurate** and **specific** information.

Feedback requires an atmosphere of sensitivity and support because most people find the deliberate request for information about themselves threatening. If I am to learn from what you tell me, if I am to really appreciate your experience of me, then I need **clear** and **direct** remarks that are not wrapped in cotton wool with all the energy drained out of them. If the feedback is coming with the best of intentions, it will be better if it arrives at me 'straight' and uncluttered, not 'packaged' for my protection.

What makes for effective feedback?

Feedback needs to be:

> *Related to specific behaviour.* There is little point in telling someone they "dominate the gathering". They need specific occasions which illustrate what is being meant. For example: "Just now, I felt that you were not really listening to what I was saying, and that you were just wanting to tell me what you think."

> *Identified as a subjective impression.* Feedback is often given as though it is a judgement from on high, delivered with all manner of claims to authority. Feedback can only be a subjective impression. For example, I cannot **know** that you are angry - though I may **believe** you are. To own the impression as a subjective one is both more honest and more productive. To say "I think you look angry: are you?" is to offer a personal impression which does not label the other person, and leaves them free to accept or reject the suggestion.

Directed toward behaviour that can be changed. To offer feedback on aspects of life that the client is powerless to change is both threatening and frustrating. For example, if someone who is self-conscious about their height is told "You look like a dwarf", this is not likely to help them listen next time.

Descriptive not evaluative. For example, it is more effective to say, "When you point your finger like that, it makes me feel as though you are treating me like a child," rather than, "Don't point your finger at me, you creep". The first describes what happened; the second makes a judgement of the client.

Well-timed. Almost always, feedback is better for being given sooner rather than later - providing the receiver is ready to hear it and there is support available.

Requested. It is most useful when the receiver has actually invited the feedback. For example, "Do you find the way I behaved just now threatening?" implies an openness of response to the feedback the individual may receive.

Checked for understanding. Check to see if what has been heard is what has been said and meant, and work at it until it is.

Feedback is a way of giving and getting help. It gives individuals an important new source of information to assist them in learning how well their behaviour matches their intentions. It increases the chances of accuracy, success and confidence in interpersonal behaviour, and helps to promote a healthy and open atmosphere of mutual regard. The free flow of constructive feedback is a powerful tool for the promotion of mutual learning.

Focusing. Focusing means bringing the client's attention to select from amongst a collection of strands those which possess most 'charge' or significance: e.g. "Which of the last few remarks seem most important to the topic we have been talking about?" It is usually experienced as a mildly challenging intervention. By use of such interventions, the counsellor exercises responsibility for maintaining some focus of interest or pursuing some theme.

Pointing out mixed messages. Clients can be alerted to discrepancies between what they say and what they do. Counsellor: "You say you feel happy about it, but you don't seem to be happy - your face is all drawn and tight..." Counsellor: "A few minutes ago you were telling me how good this relationship was, now you seem to be saying that it's too painful." Pointing out a mixed message is not intended to trap clients: if a trap is suggested to them, they will immediately become defensive.

Direct questions. Supportively asking a direct question aimed at the core of the issue - an area the client may be avoiding, concealing or hesitating in sharing - can be a useful confrontive exercise.

Challenges to personal restrictions. When **a client** celebrates **their** inability to do something they like, or has failed at something yet again - in short, when they are recycling familiar stories of failure - interruptions and mimicking their script can be sufficient for them to recognise it for what it is.

Immediacy. Immediacy, or using the 'here and now', occurs when the counsellor encourages the client to draw upon their reactions and responses to the situation they are sharing. Counsellor: "You say you always feel embarrassed when you talk about your appearance, how do you feel talking about it now?"

Being concrete. Asking for a specific or actual example can be useful. Counsellor: "Can you tell me the last time you felt lonely?"

All confrontive interventions ideally come out of a desire to assist the client and not to serve the counsellor's needs. Therefore there should be no great investment in any of them. If the observation does not fit the client, the counsellor does not have to pursue it until it does.

Cathartic Skills

The expression of strong feeling in our culture tends to be reserved for special occasions when few witnesses are present. There are strong social inhibitions about letting go of anger, grief, sadness and so on, and this can strongly restrict the choices individuals make. For example, an individual may ask for time, care and support to "talk about the loss of their parent" without realising that talking about it is only part of the process of grieving: **feeling is also part of that process.** The inhibition about experiencing such feelings fully and openly in the presence of another can give such sessions an unsatisfactory quality. There are times when clients dip in and out of feelings, unwilling or unable to choose either to express them or ignore them. Ultimately it must be the client who decides, but the counsellor's own willingness and experience in working with feelings of anger and distress will come to play a very great part in the client's decision. It seems unlikely you can ever take anyone to places you haven't at least visited yourself in emotional terms.

Physical support. Physical contact is another area of social taboos. Who can touch who where and in what circumstances is a matter full of variables. However, in counselling what is being acknowledged is the human need for contact at times of acute crisis. The holding of a hand, or an arm or a shoulder can simply tell the client that they are not alone.

Validation. To share strong feeling is a considerable risk, appreciation and respect for having taken the risk, gentle encouragement and support as it happens are ways to validate the client.

Critical scene descriptions. The client can be invited to relive some traumatic scene by retelling the events from within the present tense to evoke the unfinished and incomplete elements of the original experience.

Psychodrama. The client can be invited to return to an earlier occasion and say all the things not said at the time as though the person or group were present now.

Associations. When people begin to speak of emotionally laden events, their attention may switch, signs of feeling may become apparent on their face, breathing may become more rapid and shallower, and so on. Inviting the client to share the thought image or words they might be hearing internally can enable them to more fully experience the emotion.

Contradictions. Simply asking the client to repeat the opposite of a negative statement can have a powerful effect and can bring to the surface material to work with. For example, if a client says 'Life is just a waste of time', the contradiction 'Life is wonderful' is much more likely to bring to their awareness what the original statement actually hides.

Facilitating Change

It seems from the evidence provided by research studies that to facilitate helping it is important to:

Communicate in such a way that the client feels able to trust.

Communicate clearly and unambiguously so as to be aware that behaviour matches intentions and to know how to handle feelings.

Have a genuinely positive attitude toward the client.

Be able to be mature enough to allow the client their separateness and to respect your own, so that you do not become engulfed by their fear or overwhelmed by their grief.

Enter fully and sensitively into the world of feelings and meanings and accept the client as they express it.

Behave in a way which provides the safety for growth. The more free from threat the client feels, the more attention there is available to

deal with the feelings of conflict in the client.
Respect the client's ability to make choices even and especially when they differ from those you might like to suggest.

"The degree to which I can create relationships which facilitate the growth of others is a measure of the growth I have achieved for myself", says Carl Rogers (1961).

Chapter Twenty-one

Personal Problem-Solving

People in the helping professions often refer to the difficulties of those seeking help as 'personal problems' in a loose kind of way, well aware that not all the difficulties people experience are either 'personal' in the sense that they have their origin in decisions the clients have made for themselves or 'problems' in the sense that they have a clear solution. In what sense is the loss of a parent a problem? It is rather a naturally occurring life-crisis which the majority of people will one day have to face. Some people will meet this and other crises with little or no need of outside support; others will not. This is not a judgement upon those who at times of crisis seek out a listening ear to help them shape their experience into understanding. Some people are fortunate to live in a network of support that is freely available, but many people have no such network. In times of difficulty they are without close contacts to share their difficulties and must look outside for support. It is often the case that people who are seeking help find it difficult to request it openly and may offer a more tangible and practical need as the reason for seeking help in the beginning. In such cases, helpers need to be alert to clues which might suggest that other issues or concerns are present and to provide opportunities for the client to broach them.

Even when an individual experiences a dilemma, issue or concern in their life as a problem - for example, the desire to lose weight, give up smoking, and so on - such problems may not be capable of solution in a straightforward fashion, as the suggestion to 'eat less' to someone with a weight problem immediately demonstrates.

When someone says they 'Don't know what to do.' They are really saying that they have no **reference system** for making a choice. They have not got a secure enough base upon which to make a selection.

A reference system for making decisions about whether to stay in a relationship, or whether to buy a new house, or to change your job, will not necessarily be the same. However, most people use the same strategy to make all their decisions, or they try to. This will mean they will be good at deciding some things (things which are related to the kind of activity that the strategy was at first developed to help with) and not others. They are unlikely to know why this is so, or even to realise that there are a range of activities or decisions for which the strategy serves them well, since the development of such a strategy is largely unconscious and related to underlying beliefs. They will then use the same strategy over and over again – until it works – a sure way to perpetuate failure; since if it didn't work the first time, then it won't on the fifty third either. *If at first you don't succeed – then do something else.*

If, for example, you use pictures from your past to determine what you do in the future, then you are likely to condemn yourself to living out the same kinds of relationships and to make the same kinds of choices you have made in the past. You may then be doing little but repeating the past in slightly different versions. Such a strategy can be useful for solving conceptual problems and planning things, but it is not a useful way of solving people problems, especially if you don't want to end up in the same place again.

Information overload

When people confess to not knowing what to do in a particular situation, it is not that they lack the kind of information they need, despite what they might say. Usually, they have more information than they could ever hope to need. Most people interested in dieting, for example, know too much about diets and calories, for their own good. It is simply that *such information is not crucial to solving **their** problem.* What they lack is not information, but a way of knowing how to evaluate it usefully in relation to the outcome they are seeking.

The Importance of Context

All problems occur within some context. *The context is determined by what an individual decides to pay attention to and what they 'screen out';* and what people pay attention to is determined by what they value. When people don't know what to do, they do not know what to value out of what they have to work with. *Meaning lies in people and people code their experiences differently.* We may all experience the same event, but each of us will represent it differently in unique internal patterns. *There is a tremendous difference between an experience and how it is represented,* very much like the difference between the meal and the menu you use to order from. For most of the time, people are responding not to what is actually 'out there' in the world, but to what they think it might mean, what it 'should' mean, or what they believe they 'ought' to do about it. They continually look for what is the same in **this** experience compared to the past and not for what is novel and different.

Effective decision making however, is about choice. To have only one option is to be no more than a robot. Two alternatives equals a dilemma and is like operating with an on/off switch. Only when you have three possibilities does choice begin. **One way of defining choice is 'a multiple response to the same stimuli'.** For most of us, most of the time, choice is about having a range of ways to go after what we want. **Choice is related to Outcomes.**

Outcome

This places an emphasis upon knowing clearly and unambiguously what it is you want – *the outcome you are aiming to fulfil.* This requires stating it accurately and specifically, because sloppy language produces sloppy results. 'The best person for the job' can bring you a lot of surprises, if you don't define 'best' any more carefully than that. Once you have a clear outcome, you have to have the behavioral resources to gain it – this requires **behavioural flexibility** – which is often limited by underlying beliefs and concerns that are not always consciously known.

Most personal problems have some function or purpose in the total life circumstances of that individual. Somehow and at some time it made sense to acquire whatever habit or behaviour pattern they now seek to change. If change were such a simple and straight forward matter, helpers would quickly be out of business. The fact is that problems give people certain kinds of **secondary rewards:** ways of getting certain kinds of attention that are extremely important to them and which they believe they can not get in other ways. If, for example, I am repeatedly complaining of my ill-health and it gets me noticed, although I may complain of it a great deal of the time, I nevertheless remain heavily invested in staying the way I am, since it gets me something that I want - time, sympathy and attention.

Making technical suggestions to solve a personal problem is the least difficult aspect of helping. More important is establishing what the pay-off of the problem is and finding better ways for the client to get the same reward more safely and more effectively.

Assumptions

There are a variety of approaches that have been designed to help individuals solve personal problems. Many are recent in origin and derive from techniques developed in the 'new therapies'. The approach outlined here is based upon a learning and information model.

The underlying assumptions are:

> People can learn to solve their own problems, and when they do, they acquire skills transferable to other situations.

> Many people lack sufficient information in their awareness to solve their problems. The role of the helper is to help the person with the difficulty to raise the information into their awareness so they can act for themselves.

> Many problems are capable of improvement through the help of another.

Such an approach would not be suitable for dealing with long-standing emotional difficulties or critically serious disruptions to an individual's life, unless it were accompanied by skilled specialist help. It is important, therefore, for anyone undertaking the role of helper to ask themselves if they possess the necessary skills to help and if this approach is suitable for the problem.

Force-field analysis is an additional resource for personal problem-solving and draws on the work of Kurt Lewin (1946) and Gerard Egan (1975).

Identifying the Problem

It may be unfortunate, but it is true that the only behaviour you can do something about is your own. You cannot change other people: you can only help them to change if they want to. The problem may appear to be centred in someone else, but the only parts you can act upon immediately are the parts that influence and affect yourself. Once you have taken the first step and begun to concentrate upon your own behaviour, you can begin to apply the steps below.

Problem Solving and Decision Making Strategy

Identify the problem?

Express the essence of the problem in a simple sentence that a seven year old would understand. Keep at this stage until you get it. This may mean facing there is not one problem, but several all wrapped up in a situation. Then you have to decide which 'bit' you are going to tackle first.

What have you done so far?

Briefly outline the strategies attempted and the results obtained, so far. Explore when the individual first became aware of the issue and what were the signals that it was an issue? What are the signals that they notice now, which indicate that the problem is about to appear? (This is about finding out what the lead-up to the problem is.)

What have you not done but could attempt?

Explore alternative options and ask, non judgmentally, why they have not been attempted, or if they have, what happened? This is to begin identifying the underlying restrictions of belief.

What gets in the way?

What are the factors that hold the person back?
What might you be saying to yourself that limits you?
What other self-imposed limitations might there be that you might need to explore.
(Reference to the Personal Myths of the individual may help.)

What do you want?

What is the outcome sought in solving this problem?

Keep on going with this, until you have a positive and specific description that you are clear is potentially achievable by the person concerned.

It has to be capable of achievement by themselves and, one achieved, sustained by themselves.

Is it realistic?

How does this outcome stand up to rigorous analysis in the light of potential experience?

Modify the plan and do more work, rather than allow the person to go out and discover more pain and frustration.

Reduce it to manageable chunks:

Reduce the overall aim to manageable time-related pieces.
Make sure the time scale is realistic.

Implementation:

First steps put into effect – by when?
Ensure there is sufficient support – if needed.
Consider what will happen if the unexpected appears and confounds your efforts.

Evaluate

Review the actual events against your expectations. Invite feedback.

P:	Pose the problem accurately.
R:	Refine the problem areas into manageable chunks.
O:	Outline the 'right' kind of questions to ask.
B:	Bring back the data.
L:	Look for solutions.
E:	Evaluate options.
M:	Make a decision.
S:	So what next?

The Three Components

To solve any problem successfully, you require as much reliable information as you can get.

There are three aspects to the solution of any problem. There is a **knowing** component (what you think) a **feeling** component (how you feel about the way things are), and an **action** component (doing something about it). Most of the time it is very much easier to gather the information than it is to act upon it, and the way a person feels about things will have great influence upon what they decide to do.

Knowing

To gain information quickly, it is often better to seek someone who already knows the information you require than to try to do it all by yourself. But make sure the source of the information you seek is reliable. It is your responsibility to ensure that the information is accurate and relevant to your needs.

Ask yourself:

What do you already know about the problem?

What do you need to know?

How could you find out?

Who might be able to help?

Feeling

Having information relating to a problem does not always lead to an individual taking positive action. The evidence connecting cigarette smoking and lung cancer is in itself not sufficient to actually stop many people from smoking, though it probably makes most people think harder about giving it up or guilty if they continue. For some people, to admit that they have a particular problem would be to lose self-respect or self-esteem. Denying the problem is a way of avoiding having to confront the implications and the challenge to an individual's self-image. Alcoholics often refuse to admit they have a 'drink' problem until it is acute and therefore harder to change. Sometimes solving a problem is resisted or avoided because the person concerned would then have to consider what to do instead of complaining or feeling sorry for themselves.

Ask yourself:

How do you feel about the problem?

Do you feel that way at other times?

How important is it to you to solve the problem?

What effect would it have upon your life if you were without it?

Acting

Knowing all that is required to solve a problem and then becoming motivated only gets one to the starting-point. A problem is only solved by **doing** something about it. It is important to identify the sequence of activities and skills required to achieve a solution, and to isolate those which are most difficult or require most support or practice before trying them out.

Once those behaviours which are most difficult or most risky have been identified, they can be practised away from the situation until confidence has been developed and until the person feels easier in trying them out in the real situation. Talking is a form of practice, and so is role-play. The advantage of this kind of practice is that it provides an opportunity to evaluate the results in a risk-free environment which allows you to modify anything with which you are not satisfied.

Reviewing

Stay involved. Once you have put a plan into action, it is important to check how you went about it so that you can remember it next time or go over the areas of difficulty. Reviewing enables people to build upon their success and to identify skills they already have and use.

Force-field Analysis as a Problem-solving Method

Force-field analysis can be used when working with someone on a problem they wish to change. It provides a step-by-step approach that covers all the factors in the situation, including those which promote change and are therefore helpful, and those which oppose change and are therefore restraining.

(i)   *Identify the Problem*

* Is the problem owned by the client? (Are they willing to take responsibility for the problem?)
* Is the problem soluble? (Is the problem expressed in concrete terms understood by both parties?)

(ii)   *Clarify the Problem*

* Break down the problem into sub-parts and explore their interaction.

(iii)   Establish Priorities

* Choose a 'chunk' of the problem to begin with which can be handled easily. Ensure that it is under the control of the person being helped.

(iv)   Establish a Workable Goal

* State the object in a behaviourally descriptive way that ensures that you will have indicators of its achievement.
* Ensure that the client owns the goal and is committed to attaining it, and is not merely saying so to keep you quiet.
* Break the goals down into workable units.

(v) *Means to Achieve the Goals*

* Look at all those forces, however incidental, that may well facilitate and encourage the client to achieve change. Include internal approval, success, external praise, environmental support etc. Do the same for all those factors which will undermine, inhibit or restrain the client from moving ahead easily. Put this into two columns as below:

Facilitating	Restraining
1.	1.
2.	2.
3.	3.

Developing a Behavioural Strategy

In identifying a strategy of change, it is important to remember the principles of behaviour change - shaping (approximation to the desired performance), avoidance, reinforcement - and the lack of usefulness of punitive or negative support for failure.

Implementation

Gain a clear contract of commitment to achieve specific goals in an agreed time.

Evaluation

Revise the information and include unintended as well as expected outcomes.

Agree success

Or check where things went wrong.

References

Avila, D.L., Combs, A.W., and Purkey, W.L.: **The Helping Relationship Source Book.** Vols. I & II. Boston, Mass.: Allyn & Bacon, 1977.

Bandler, J., and Grinder: **Frogs into Princes.** Real People Press., 1976.

Carkhuff, R.R.: **The Development of Human Resources.** New York: Holt Rinehart, 1971.

Coombs, A.W.: **Studies in the Helping Professions.** Florida: 1969.

Egan, G.: **The Skilled Helper: a Model for Systematic Helping and Interpersonal Relating.** Wandsworth, 1975.

Fielder, **F.E.: 'The Concept of the Ideal Therapeutic Relationship'.** Journal of Consulting Psychology, Volume 14., 195), pp. 239-245.

Heron, J.: **Six Category Intervention Analysis.** Guildford: Department of Adult Education, University of Surrey, 1976.

Jourard, S.: **The Transparent Self.** Princeton, New Jersey: Van Nostrand, 1964 (revised edition 1971).

Pietrofesa, J.J., Hoffman, A., Spekte, H.J., and Pinto, D.V.: **Counselling, Theory, Research and Practice.** Chicago: Rand McNally, 1978.

Rogers, C.R.: **On Becoming a Person.** Boston: Houghton Mifflin, 1961.

Truax, C.B., and Carkhuff, R.R.: **Toward Effective Counselling and Psychotherapy.** Chicago: Aldine, 1967.

Select Bibliography

Halmos, P.: **The Faith of the Counsellors.** London: Constable, 1978.

Heron, J.: **Helping the Client.** London. Sage, 1991.

Kopp, S.: **If you Meet the Buddah on the Road, Kill Him!** London. Sheldon Press, 1974.

Miller, J.C.: **Tutoring**. London: Further Education Curriculum Review and Development Unit, 1982.

Peck, M. Scott.: **The Road Less Travelled.** London: Arrow, 1990.

Rowan, J.: **The Reality Game.** London: Routledge Kegan Paul, 1983.

Rowan, J.: **Feeling and Personhood.** London. Sage, 1992.

Vaughan, F.: **The Inward Arc.** London. Shambhala, 1985.